CHAPTER 4

CHAPTER 5

CHAPTER 6

CHAPTER 7

Mazatzal Peak
(7,888 ft.)

MAZATZAL WILDERNESS

Bushnell Tanks

FOUR PEAKS WILDERNESS

TONTO NATIONAL FOREST

ROOSEVELT LAKE

SUPERSTITION WILDERNESS

REAVIS CREEK

Superior

GLOBE

Oracle

Summerhaven

Mount Lemmon
(9,157 ft.)

Sabino Canyon

Manning Camp

CORONADO NATIONAL FOREST

SAGUARO NATIONAL PARK

Kentucky Camp

Patagonia

MT. WRIGHTSON WILDERNESS

Mt. Wrightson
(9,453 ft.)

Parker Canyon Lake

CORONADO NATIONAL FOREST

WILDERNESS

terminus of the Arizona Trail

CIENEGA CREEK

Tucson

SAGUARO NATIONAL PARK

SANTA CRUZ RIVER

NOGALES

Nogales

O

N

A

M

E

X

I

C

GILA RIVER

VERDE RIVER

SALT RIVER

PHOENIX

CASA GRANDE

SANTA CRUZ RIVER

BUCKEYE

GILA BEND

WICKENBURG

SONOITA

Along *the* Arizona Trail

◆◆◆◆◆◆◆◆◆◆◆

PHOTOGRAPHY BY
Jerry Sieve

STORIES BY
M. John Fayhee

WESTCLIFFE PUBLISHERS

ENGLEWOOD, COLORADO

To the memory of my mom—Marjorie Martin Morris—
who not only allowed me to wander when I was young, but encouraged, even demanded, that I do so.
—M. John Fayhee

ISBN: 1-56579-276-9

Photographs copyright, 1998 Jerry Sieve. All rights reserved.
Text copyright, 1998 M. John Fayhee. All rights reserved.
Illustrations copyright, 1998 Asa Battles. All rights reserved

Designer: Paula Schlosser Design
Map designer: John Wagner
Production manager: Harlene Finn
Editor: Cat Ohala

Published by Westcliffe Publishers, Inc.
PO Box 1261
Englewood, Colorado 80150

Printed in Hong Kong through Palace Press International

LIBRARY OF CONGRESS CATALOGING-IN-PUBLICATION DATA
Sieve, Jerry.
    Along the Arizona Trail / photography by Jerry Sieve ; text by M.
John Fayhee.
        p.   cm.
    ISBN 1-56579-276-9
    1. Arizona Trail—Pictorial works. 2. Arizona Trail—Description
and travel. 3. Arizona—Description and travel. 4. Hiking—Arizona
Trail. 5. Sieve, Jerry—Journeys—Arizona Trail. I. Fayhee, M.
John, 1955-   . II. Title.
F815.S57   1998
917.9104'33—dc21   98-15261
                                                 CIP

*For more information about other fine books and calendars from Westcliffe Publishers, please
call your local bookstore, contact us at 1-800-523-3692, or write for our free color catalog.*

FIRST FRONTISPIECE: *Evening light in the Superstition Wilderness, Tonto National Forest*
SECOND FRONTISPIECE: *View from East Rim overlook, Kaibab National Forest*

ACKNOWLEDGMENTS

An awful lot of people went out of their way to one degree or another to make certain that my two-month hike along the Arizona Trail (AZT) went as smoothly as possible. Among them I would specifically like to thank Dale Shewalter, the visionary who first conceived the AZT, and Eric Smith, AZT Trail Steward, who graciously spent about twelve years on the phone helping me plan my AZT hike. Also, I would like to thank Tom Folks of the Bureau of Land Management (BLM), John Neiling of the United States Forest Service (USFS), Kim Crumbo of the National Park Service (NPS), Joel McCurry (USFS), Billy Cardasco (Babbitt Ranches), John Nelson (USFS), Paul Jones (City of Flagstaff), David Michael (USFS), Don Muise (USFS), Rob Ingram (USFS), Art Wirtz (USFS), Brad Orr (USFS), Greg Hansen (USFS), Stuart Herkenhoff (USFS), Jim Martin (AZT Trail Steward), Dale Mance (USFS), Dwayne Moates (NPS), Steve Anderson (Pima County Parks and Recreation Department), Dorothy Morgan (BLM), Steve Goldman (USFS), Cathy Kahlow (USFS), and Steve Saway (Huachuca Hiking Club) for taking the time to lead me through the AZT via map over the phone.

A big set of hugs and kisses to my wife, Gay Gangel-Fayhee, for keeping the bill collectors at bay and for taking care of my dog while I was on the trail. Special thanks to Catherine Carson; Fosco Spinedi; David and Suzanne Wright; Joseph and Aileen Fayhee; Frank, Laurie, and Emily Hogg; Jay Scott; and Allan West for helping with logistics and/or providing a safe haven while I was on the trail. And, for about the billionth (and, I swear, the very last) time, thanks to my bosses at Eagle-Summit Publishing, Bob Brown and Michael Kirschbaum, for allowing me to wander away from my desk for months at a time. Along those lines, a hearty pat on the back to Tom Jones and Renee Aragon for keeping the publications I edit in business while I was gone.

A big thanks to Dwight J. Ohala for taking the time to verify the spelling of watuzi. Also, I would like to thank Vasque for the boots, Garmin for the global positioning system, and Phil Huff for the use of the cellular phone, which made ordering pizza while I was on the trail much easier.

—M. John Fayhee

CONTENTS

PREFACE

◆◆◆◆◆◆◆◆◆◆◆◆◆

TRAVELING SOUTH ON Interstate 10, I have just passed Tucson on my way to southern Arizona's wonderful grassland areas. I'm on another image-making trip for the "Trail book," as it has become known in my household. After driving more than three hours, something has now occurred to me as I pass through the heart of Arizona's major development areas: I have been traveling through smog for more than 150 miles! Eventually, as I get farther from Tucson, the skies begin to clear and become the rich blue for which Arizona is so famous. On reaching my destination at Montezuma Pass in Coronado National Memorial, which is within several miles of the southern terminus of the Arizona Trail (AZT), no hint of smog remains. The air is clear and clean, and the light has that snappy, crisp look seen so often in the Southwest.

My trip has become a metaphor for what the AZT is all about. Visiting this wonderful pathway can help people feel like they have returned to a time when all of Arizona was one vast, untamed wilderness. By leaving the smog and developed areas, you also depart from the "progress" that is taking place so rapidly. Developers are out of control in Arizona. Having lived here for almost twenty-five years now, I have seen it happen again and again. The usual scenario is one in which the developers come in, commit a kind of scorched-earth policy, and then they are gone. The AZT is an antidote to this fact of life in late-twentieth century Arizona.

How did Arizona look when humans first visited this region of the earth? *Walk the trail.* How can a person reflect on our "progress" as a species? *Walk the trail.* Want to experience a little bit of what truly wild creatures experience? *Walk the trail.*

The AZT is not just a vertical line that crosses our state from one end to the other; it is also a vertical trail. Elevations along the trail currently range from about 2,000 to 9,000 feet. When the trail is completed, it will reach an elevation of 12,000 feet. This means that visitors will see just about every ecological zone in Arizona—from lower Sonoran desert to alpine tundra. This is equivalent to traveling from Sonora, Mexico, to Northern Canada.

This book is more than just a collection of images of the trail. Rather, it is images of the areas and ecological regions through which the trail passes. Broadening the scope of the areas covered allowed me to celebrate photographically the multitude of life zones and almost surreal landscapes that the AZT traverses.

At the end of another day's work photographing for the book, I was hiking down a forested trail listening to the squeak, squeak, squeak my backpack makes while I walk. The light was low and soon it would be gone. I usually keep my eyes down as I hike at this time of day so that I don't trip over something on the trail. I happened to look up and there, in the middle of the trail less than 50 feet away, was a coyote. I stopped in my tracks—as did the coyote—and we both stood and stared at each other for what seemed quite a long time. What was he thinking? Was he waiting to see if I was going to attack him? Or was he saying to himself: *What is this guy doing here? This is my territory.* I guess we both belong on this trail. Or rather, humans *need* to be on the trail. We need to be able to get away and learn to be a little bit more like a coyote.

—*Jerry Sieve*
photographer

◆◆◆

Aspen and fir during an early snowstorm, San Francisco Peaks

INTRODUCTION

◆.◆.◆.◆.◆.◆.◆.◆.◆.◆..◆

SOMETIME DURING THE MID 1970s, when I first was commencing my love affair with the American West, I found myself eyeballing a road map of Arizona, the border of which lay only 20 miles from my home in southwest New Mexico. It did not take long to notice that the Grand Canyon State was covered near 'bout top to bottom with great green swatches of Forest Service land. With only a few gaps, it looked like it would be possible to hike from Utah all the way down to Mexico without ever leaving those green swatches—an intriguing possibility for a died-in-the-wool long-distance backpacker; but, sad to say, a possibility I never explored further.

A few years ago, I learned that a man named Dale Shewalter had not only thought about the possibility of hiking from Utah to Mexico, through the heart of Arizona, but had acted on that thought. Ever since he moved to Arizona in 1974, Shewalter, a fifth-grade teacher who now lives near Flagstaff, had been intrigued by the long-distance hiking opportunities that his adopted home state boasted in spades.

In 1982 Shewalter hiked from Mogollon, New Mexico, to the Mogollon Rim, near Flagstaff, to sort of show himself (if not the world) that it was possible to link up long backpacking routes in Arizona.

"That trip confirmed my belief that long-distance hiking was possible here," Shewalter told me one crisp October day in Flagstaff. "I started thinking about planning a south-north route from Mexico to Utah. I knew we had plenty of existing trails in Arizona; all we lacked was connections."

In 1985 Shewalter started working on establishing those connections. He had some friends drop him off at Nogales, on the Mexican border, and he hiked all the way to Fredonia, a stone's throw from Kanab, Utah. The hike took two months.

"During that hike, I established a workable corridor for a continuous trail from Mexico to Utah," Shewalter told me. "It worked out well enough that the current Arizona Trail corridor pretty much follows the route I hiked."

In late summer 1985 Shewalter presented the idea for his border-to-border trail to the Arizona Hiking and Equestrian Trails Committee, a support group for nonmotorized trails that has since evolved into the Arizona State Committee on Trails.

"They enthusiastically embraced the idea," Shewalter remembers. "They almost immediately took on the concept of the Arizona Trail as a goal. In late 1986, we started making specific plans with the Forest Service, as well as several other government agencies."

In 1988 Shewalter took a year-long leave of absence from his teaching job to work on the Arizona Trail (AZT) full time. Later that year the first section of the AZT—part of the existing Kaibab Plateau Trail north of the Grand Canyon—was dedicated.

During the next few years, Arizona State Parks started working diligently on the trail, establishing several intergovernmental agreements and hiring a full-time AZT trail steward. Things really got moving in 1993 when the nonprofit Arizona Trail Association was established.

"Ever since then, things have been moving pretty fast," Shewalter said.

IN LATE 1996 I DECIDED TO send off for a packet of AZT information. Within a few weeks I had received several reams of skinny, and poring over that skinny began to consume me. In a ritual that has pretty much defined my twelve-plus years of marriage, my wife, Gay, began to roll her eyes and shake her head as my AZT file/pile began to get thicker

◆.◆.◆

Early morning along Cienega Creek, Empire-Cienega Ranch Conservation Area

and higher. With the Appalachian and Colorado trails already under my belt, as well as the 750-mile Colorado section of the Continental Divide Trail, Gay knew that yet another long-distance hiking storm was about to break in the middle of her otherwise tranquil life.

Finally, she came out and asked when I planned to leave for the AZT. "Maybe in the fall," I replied sheepishly, hoping against hope not to be served with divorce papers right then and there.

On October 5, 1997, I began a two-month hike along the AZT from the Utah border near, well, near nothing, to Coronado National Memorial on the faraway Mexican border. This book is a result of that trek.

A COUPLE OF NOTES ABOUT my AZT hike. The goal of the Arizona Trail Foundation is to dedicate the AZT by the year 2000. The trail will end up being somewhere around 750 miles long when completed. When I hit the trail, about 550 miles were up and running, although some parts were more up and running than others. The AZT that I hiked consisted of sections of perfectly coiffed and well-marked trail, unmarked trail, overgrown and unmaintained trail that scarcely deserved to be *called* trail, dirt roads, paved roads, and hypothetical trail corridors that headed off into the woods. There were also several sections where no trail corridor yet existed.

All told, I ended up hiking about 650 miles—meaning that I hiked about 100 miles via dirt road or cross-country through places where there was not yet official trail of any species, but those miles were located more or less where the AZT will one day be. There were a couple of gaps in my hike, places where the trail, in 1997, was little more than a glimmer in some planner's eye, places where even the most general idea of where the AZT would pass had not yet been determined. I could have linked my way, again, along dirt roads and cross-country through those sections for the sake of continuity, but I'm getting too old and decrepit to lose sleep about theoretical continuity. I'll go back and finish those sections when the trail corridor has been identified.

That said, I have often been asked what possessed me to embark on my AZT hike two-plus years before the trail was scheduled to be completed. This marks the third long hike I have taken on a trail that was mostly done,

but still had a long way to go. I find hiking along nascent trails to be exciting and compelling. I enjoy having to use my maps, compass, Global Positioning System (GPS), and wits to make my way from one point to another point many hundreds of miles away. I like hiking long sections of trail that lack signage, and others that lack tread all together. Although this is an easy thing to say while sitting in a comfortable office, I like having the fear of getting lost looming above me like a circling, drooling vulture. Helps keep the arteries flowing free. It's controlled exploration in an era when pure, honest exploration is all but impossible. Besides, when you hike a trail that is not yet complete, it gives you bragging rights over all those who follow. "You think the Arizona Trail is difficult *now*, you should have been here back when I hiked it . . . "

I decided to hike north to south because it was easier for me to get two months off from work in the fall than in the spring, and climate necessitates a Utah-to-Mexico itinerary if you're hiking the AZT in autumn. In early October, temperatures in southern Arizona are too hot for arduous hiking, and by the end of November there's tons of snow on the ground in the northern part of the state. My goal was to get down below the Mogollon Rim before winter hit full blast, but not to get to the southern part of the state too early.

As Shewalter indicated, the AZT was conceived as a south-to-north route—the idea being that if you leave the Mexican border along about March 1, you can follow the spring flower bloom all the way to Utah. I had the wonderful chance to experience the seasonal flip side of the design consciousness: By hiking north to south, I had the chance to view fall foliage for two straight months.

The next thing that needs mentioning is the water issue. For planning purposes, the Arizona Trail Association has printed a series of 34 informational "section sheets" that cover the entire trail. These section sheets, I should note, are different from the "passage sheets," which are designed for trail users rather than planners. Each of the section sheets includes the name of a person, usually a Forest Service employee, who can be called for more information. Since, at the time of my hike, no guidebook to the AZT yet existed, I opted to call all of those contacts while planning my itinerary. Almost without exception I was asked what I planned on doing about water.

I usually responded that I planned to take advantage of the myriad springs, stock tanks, rivers, and lakes listed on my maps. Invariably I was told that such-and-such a lake was as dry as a bone, such-and-such a spring hadn't had water in it for years, and such-and-such a stock tank held water so skanky that even cows wouldn't go near it—if it held water at all.

In short, it became apparent that I would have to stash water caches along the route, something I've never had to do before. I realized early on in the planning process that things would be a lot easier on the logistics front if I had my truck with me while on the AZT. Strange thing, that realization, as I usually don't bring my truck with me on hikes. Quite the opposite. As much as I love my truck, one of the things I love most about long-distance hiking is that I can spend several months away from vehicles. After finishing each section of trail, I would have to arrange for a shuttle to go back and get my truck at the last town. Then I would have to shuttle the truck ahead to the next town.

All told, the logistics for my AZT hike ended up being somewhat complex, as not only did I need to cache water, but later I had to go back in and remove those caches. Thus, most places on the AZT I visited not once, not twice, but three times: when I placed the water cache, when I hiked through the area, and when I returned to remove said caches. This ended up being a lot more tiring than the hike itself.

The good part about this system was that, since I was placing water caches, I decided that I might as well place food and fuel caches at the same time. Therefore, I never had to carry more than three days worth of food and fuel, which is unprecedented for a hike of this duration. Not only did this mean I could carry a less heavy pack, but it meant I could stash food that was at least one culinary notch above my usual backpacking fare. Rather than surviving for two months on instant rice mixed with instant soup, I could enjoy instant rice mixed with instant soup *and* canned chicken.

By the time this book sees print, the AZT route that I hiked will no longer be the AZT. At least two new trail segments—one near Roosevelt Lake and another between Flagstaff and the Mogollon Rim—are scheduled to be opened by early 1998. Such will be the case for several more years, as this is a trail that is experiencing some serious momentum. It is metamorphosing minute by minute.

By the turn of the century, the AZT will take its place as one of the best trails in the country. It was a pleasure and a privilege to rub elbows with it for two of the most splendid months of my life.

My hat's definitely off to the people of Arizona for having the foresight and energy to build such a trail.

—M. John Fayhee
Mad Spinner of Tales

Utah Border *to the* South Rim *of the* Grand Canyon

◆◆◆◆◆◆◆◆◆◆◆◆◆

WHEN IT COMES TO LONG JOURNEYS and adventures, I generally prefer endings to beginnings or middles. The have-done has always been infinitely more appealing to me than the about-to-do or the am-doing. This is not to say that I do not appreciate the stomach-fluttering thrill of getting ready to embark upon adventures or actually participating in those adventures; but, for the most part, I always long most for the time when I return from the boonies to my real life, my body lean and mean, and my cranial mainframe overflowing with yarns that, once the journey is done, can ferment freely and grow, unencumbered by the inconvenience of reality, and can be related time and time again to my increasingly exasperated amigos.

Long ago I stopped my self-analysis on this obvious personality defect. It's just the way I am. But it dawned on me as I was beginning the thousand-foot ascent of the Kaibab Plateau—my very first steps along the Arizona Trail (AZT)—while the scorching desert sun was breaking over the stunningly beautiful, heat-shimmering Vermillion Cliffs, which dominated the entire eastern horizon, that for the first time in memory I was savoring every molecule, every morsel of the beginning of a trip, rather than wishing mightily for that beginning to soon become a thing of the past.

During the two years I planned my hike along the AZT, I found myself getting giddy with anticipation, rather than overwhelmed with trepidation.

Certainly, much of this prehike eagerness stemmed from the simple fact that I was going to be away from the rigors of workaday life for two whole months. But there was more to it than that. Although I was pretty familiar with Arizona, having traveled quite a bit through the Grand Canyon State over the years, I knew that the AZT would take me through territory that was not only among the most astounding and exotic on the planet, but at the same time it was territory that was totally foreign to me. For the most part I would be hiking for 750 miles through personal terra incognita—and that excited me beyond belief. I couldn't have been more tickled if I had been planning a trip to Timbuktu.

I had a jauntiness to my stride as I made my way up the side of the Kaibab Plateau. And that jauntiness, I am happy to report, lasted for almost a full hour, until the heat of the day starting fusing my parched tongue to the roof of my arid mouth. Even though it was still well before mid-morning snack time, the intensity of the temperature caught me with my pants down. It's not that I didn't know that Arizona would be a smidgen on the warm side; I was just stunned at how fast after sunrise the mercury exploded through the top of the thermometer. I slathered on sunblock the way a southern cook slathers Crisco on chicken.

It wasn't just the heat that I found captivating. The recent change in the weather was profound. I had arrived in Arizona three days prior to starting my hike. On the day of my arrival I had car camped near the hamlet of Jacob Lake—about 25 miles south of the Utah border—and found myself in

◆.◆.◆

Near the AZT, Kaibab National Forest

the epicenter of the most fearsome thunderstorm it has ever been my displeasure to whimper my way through. Even though I had heard from numerous people that the summer of 1997 was the wettest in living memory in northern Arizona, I simply could not believe what was happening directly above my tent. It was like a bad-dream combination of the Wizard of Oz and something straight out of one of the gnarlier parts of the Old Testament. The storm struck just after dusk. I had seen the clouds move in and had made myself comfortable in my tent. Shortly thereafter, a few pitter-patters of innocuous-seeming rain fell, then a bolt or two of lightning popped in the distance, then the wind picked up. Within minutes the climatological Spam hit the meteorological fan. If only two of the three storm components—wind, rain,

In the early morning light, the author prepares for his day on the AZT
◆◆◆

before you can even start thinking that thought, then it takes another second to finish thinking it.

That storm drenched and beat down the world. Yet, here I was three days later, on the flanks of the Kaibab Plateau, in the blazing sun, tromping through dust so dry that it seemed like water in any form had not visited this place since the last Ice Age. Things seem to change fast in Arizona. It was at this point that I started thinking of Arizona as the "state of surprises."

> "*It's not that I didn't know that Arizona would be a smidgen on the warm side; I was just stunned at how fast after sunrise the mercury exploded through the top of the thermometer.*"

lightning—would have been going on, I would have rated the weather sub-foul, but all three components were trying mightily to outdo each other. The lightning won the contest hands down. After the storm had raged for almost an hour, I started counting the flashes. I stopped counting at 500, and the storm raged for another forty minutes after that. And it was damned hard to count those bolts, as, for the most part, they were transpiring in groups of three and four. It's sobering to be lying in your little single-wall tent, counting lightning flashes by twos and threes for more than an hour. A large number of those flashes lasted so long that I had the opportunity to think, *My, that's a long one*, which is a scary thing because it takes at least a second

THE NIGHT BEFORE COMMENCING my hike along the Plateau, I car camped at the AZT's northern terminus, which was not yet an official trailhead (there were signs that there soon would be signs, but as of yet there were no signs), with my wife, Gay, and my sister-in-law, Cathy Carson, who would be driving around and meeting me every evening at designated rendezvous points between Utah and the northern rim of the Grand Canyon. Seventy-five miles of catered hiking. Life is good.

Our campsite was located right on the Utah–Arizona border in the heart of some extremely remote, Edward Abbey-esque slickrock desert, which contained all the requisite cacti, mesquite, and tarantulas a fearless hiker could ever possibly want in his immediate vicinity. We sat up until well past dusk in our shorts and T-shirts, enjoying the balminess. It was October 4, 1997, the height of late summer—Arizona style.

My plan was, as my plan always is the night before I begin a long hike, to spring out of bed eight or ten hours before dawn, assemble myself with near-military precision and bearing, and embark upon my two-month journey with a no-nonsense, unwavering gleam in my eye well before the sun broke the horizon. Not surprisingly, my first morning on the trail did not quite go like that. (It never does.) Even though I had prepared for this hike in infinite detail, I still felt frantically disorganized that first morning. As the sun made its way toward my immediate reality, I was still diddling with gear and leisurely sipping a third cup of coffee. By the time I started making my way up the Kaibab Plateau, El Sol was blasting down on me without mercy or compassion, making me pay dearly for my morning dalliance.

Because my entourage was to meet me every night for the next five days, I only had to carry a daypack for the first 70 miles of my trek, but I loaded that pack with 6 liters of water, less out of concern about keeping hydrated (although there was certainly *that*) than with the intention of carrying enough of a load to whip my pudgy posterior into something resembling trail shape before having to hike into and out of the Grand Canyon. I sucked down two of those liters before making it to the rim of the plateau.

For some idiotic reason, I decided to bring my dog, Cali, along on this first day. Cali is the toughest trail dog I have ever known; but, like her master, she is genetically programmed to dwell comfortably in the land of snow and cold. She has long, jet-black fur, and she doesn't know a cactus from an enchilada. The few times we have ever taken her into the desert, she has made a beeline toward every prickly pear, cholla, and barrel cactus in the neighborhood—with predictable results—and today was no exception.

After spending 30 minutes removing cactus needles from Cali's paws, I stood and peered eastward toward the massive Paria Plateau. I was hoping to eyeball some California condors—the continent's biggest bird—several of which have been released in the area, but there was more on my mind than pterodactyl-size birds as I gazed at the Paria. Two weeks before I began this trek, eleven people had been swept to their death by a monumental flash flood in Antelope Canyon, less than 35 miles from where I stood.

When my wife heard that news, she asked, "That's not anywhere near the Arizona Trail, is it?"

"Heck no, baby," I responded, lying through my teeth.

At least twenty people had admonished me before I left on the AZT to "keep your eyes peeled for flash floods." I assured every one of those people that I would do just that. The thing is, how on earth do you keep your eyes peeled for a flash flood? The rainstorm that produced the flood that swept away those eleven poor souls originated 30 miles upstream. The sky was clear and the slot canyon through which they were walking was perfectly dry when a 10-foot wall of water appeared instantaneously. There was no warning. I gulped, turned south, and pointed my feet toward Mexico.

Rock formations near the northern terminus of the trail

◆·◆·◆

Aspen near Little Round Valley, Kaibab National Forest

❖❖❖

Wᴀᴇɴ I sᴀʏ Cᴀʟɪ ᴀɴᴅ I ᴡᴇʀᴇ on the "trail," I am using that word very loosely. Actually, we were following a series of rough, infrequently used, unmarked jeep tracks that were passing through some of the most remote Bureau of Land Management (BLM) territory in the entire country, which is saying a mouthful. The main BLM guy responsible for establishing the trail in these parts, Tom Folks, had been kind enough to draw the approximate AZT route hereabouts onto several 7.5-minute topographic maps. "But," he warned me, "not all the dirt roads out there appear on the map. It'll be easy to get lost." I sort of brushed off his warning, telling him in no uncertain terms that a man of my infinite backpacking experience and overwhelming trail savvy would have no trouble whatsoever following the route he had marked on my maps.

AZT Lesson Number One: Always listen intently to local people-in-the-know. By 10 AM, I was neck deep in a mishmash of roads of equal primitive-

ness that presented a veritable smorgasbord of orientational options. There were no signs or trail markers of any kind, and I was having to make supposed educated guesses about every 15 feet. This is part of the beauty and the challenge of hiking a trail that is not yet complete. I mean, any putz can follow a well-marked trail. It takes a special kind of putz to attempt an end-to-end hike of a trail that does not yet fully exist.

Actually I had the ability to cheat a little because my friend Tom Jones, who had recently hiked along this section of the AZT, gave me a Global Positioning System (GPS) coordinate for a point located on a section of recently built trail that I was supposed to pass. The problem is, a GPS coordinate gives route information based on how the crow flies, not on how the crow walks. You have to figure out the best route to that coordinate for yourself. Moreover, my supposed wilderness-purist philosophy was feeling a little compromised by the whole notion of carrying a GPS—although I should point out that the exact nanosecond that the Garmin Company offered me free use of its latest twelve-channel model, I pretty much jumped at the chance to have it. I have been a starving writer for too many years to turn down free gear, whether I need it or not. Still, I had decided before I left that I would only use this contraption during dire, life-threatening emergencies. Otherwise, I would be committing a bona fide trail sin: relying on technology instead of my own wits.

Even though I was not exactly confident that I was on the AZT, I was not too worried because I only planned to hike 12 miles that first day, and since the road on which I was supposed to meet Gay and Cathy at 1 PM ran east-west, I knew that all I had to do was hike south and I would cross it at some point or another. I figured I had ample time to muddle my way through the sparse piñon and juniper woods.

Still, the farther I hiked, the more anxious about my route I became. Just as I was about to relent and sell my soul to the technological demons by using my GPS, I began a short, steep descent that, according to my map, could only be into something called "The Basin." Suddenly I felt studly, which is always a bad thing karmically. Off to my left I noticed a couple of people standing next to a pickup truck. I guessed them to be hunters, and I ambled over to see if I could find out just exactly where I was without appearing like I didn't know just exactly where I was. Before I could even mouth a casual observation about the weather, one of them asked, "Why are you hiking on the road instead of on the Arizona Trail?" That, I told her, was a very good question. It ended up that these two people were part of an AZT volunteer trail crew, and they had just, twenty seconds before, completed a new section that moseyed along directly and in short order to the GPS coordinate Tom Jones had given to me. Ended up that I had followed Tom Folks' directions perfectly. Miracle of miracles.

The best part of all this was that I became the very first AZT thru-hiker to beat feet on this brand-spanking-new stretch of trail. After walking 8

Along the trail near East Rim Viewpoint, Kaibab National Forest

◆◆◆

miles on jeep track, it was glorious to stride along on genuine footpath. The new trail zigged and zagged (as good trails do) through small washes and drainages, over little ridgetops, and finally to the exact point where I was supposed to meet my wife and sister-in-law. When I got there, Gay and Cathy were nowhere to be seen. I feared the worst—that the directions I had laid on them were bad or that the rough road had ripped the oil pan out of Gay's Subaru at the exact moment a renegade motorcycle gang passed by.

Cali and I walked a mile in the blazing midday heat to Dead Man Pockets, a small water hole I noticed on the map. I still was not comfortable about my as-yet-untested plan of placing water caches along the route. It simply did not seem like a "pure" way to hike a long trail. I wanted to see what the local water sources looked like because it was not too late to revise

> "*The new trail zigged and zagged (as good trails do) through small washes and drainages, over little ridgetops...*"

my water cache strategy. Dead Man Pockets was absolutely disgusting. It was about 10 feet across, and was more mud and cow urine than water. It would be a serious bummer to hike all day, getting thirstier and thirstier by the mile, only to arrive at a place like this. You would have to spend hours just filtering enough drinking water to survive until the next water source. And we won't even talk about how funky you would have to be before you even considered bathing in such a place.

When I got back to the trail intersection, where I had dropped my pack, Gay and Cathy drove up. They had spent the day hiking in the Paria Canyon-Vermillion Cliffs Wilderness Area. We made camp in a small clearing

View of the Vermillion Cliffs from the East Rim

◆.◆.◆

just off the road, and I spent the remainder of the afternoon sucking down water like a camel that had just crossed the Sahara in the middle of the summer. Even though I was surprisingly weary, I could not help but smile as I sat in front of my tent. I was past the about-to-do stage of my on-foot journey to Mexico and was just barely into the am-doing stage, and that felt splendid. I know it's ridiculous, maybe even idiotic, to feel any sense of accomplishment after the first of sixty trail days, but feel such a sense I did. I did not get lost in a place where, supposedly, it would have been easy to do so, and I did not wither away and die, even though it was hotter than 90°F with zero-percent humidity.

But, in the midst of my modest reverie—which, by the way, was very short lived—a hard reality began to sink in: This was going to be a long and difficult journey.

The best kind, by far.

This hike no longer existed on maps or in my imagination. It was right here, under my nose.

The next morning, I was up at 5:30 and on the trail well before the sun broke over the crest of the Vermillion Cliffs.

THE KAIBAB NATIONAL FOREST began a mile south of camp. The Kaibab Plateau Trail, which the AZT followed, began at the forest boundary. The Kaibab Plateau Trail, although not the most well-used and prominent footpath in the world, at least existed, at least on paper, at least theoretically. I was told by several Forest Service people that, if I paid attention and if I was not a complete boob, I should have no problem following this trail all the way to Grand Canyon National Park.

"*This was going to be a long and difficult journey. The best kind, by far.*"

Since I was not carrying a full pack, I decided to start pounding out relatively big miles right out of the chute on this hike. So on my second day out, I had 15.5 miles scheduled, which I figured (while I was planning my itinerary four months earlier back in the comfort of my home) would be no problem whatsoever, since I would have this nice trail to tromp upon. I left Cali with Gay and Cathy. They were to meet me at US Highway 89A, 3 miles east of Jacob Lake and a stone's throw from the place I was camping when that hideous storm passed directly over me.

There was nice trail to the National Forest boundary where, to my unbelieving eyes, there suddenly was trail no more. It flat out ended. I clambered over a wooden fence and scratched my noggin in disbelief. I walked back and forth along the fence several times, and there simply was no trail that I could see. AZT Lesson Number Two: Never take anything for granted—*ever*.

I spent thirty minutes searching for the trail before giving up. There was a dirt road heading straight south and, according to my maps, that road would take me almost exactly to the point where I was supposed to meet Gay and Cathy. I was sorely disappointed. The road had nary a curve as far as the eye could see. It undulated up and down, and traversed shadeless terrain for mile after mile. By mid morning, my brow caked with dried sweat, I could stand it no longer. There simply had to be a trail nearby. I climbed over a barbed-wire fence, dropped my pack in the shade, and began an earnest search for hike-able tread. It simply galls me when I can't locate a trail that I've been told exists. No luck. The best I could do was to find a ratty jeep track that headed mostly south. I decided to follow it because, even if it eventually led me to Abilene, at least it passed through shady and cool ponderosa woods.

Several times the track petered out and I had to bushwhack until I stumbled upon another old road. This I did about forty-three times, until I fully expected at any moment to come across a small village where people were wearing fur hats and speaking Ukrainian. I knew I was heading more or less in the right direction, but all these jeep tracks were meandering enough that I had no idea whether I would eventually come out on Highway 89A, 3 or 14 miles east of Jacob Lake. My stomach was starting to

The author signs in at a trailhead marker by Jacob Lake, Kaibab Plateau

GAY GANGEL-FAYHEE

◆◆◆

churn. Then I passed what surely had to be Government Reservoir (which boasted nary a drop of moisture)—meaning, once again, I was where I was supposed to be. But, if such was the case, where was the damned trail? Once more, I dropped my pack and searched in vain.

At this point I picked up a more defined dirt road and, shortly thereafter, passed a dirt road intersection marked Forest Road 49/Forest Road 49A. Again, right on target. I was making good time despite my circuitous tour of every long-abandoned logging road in northern Arizona. After an hour I passed another dirt road intersection, this one marked Forest Road 49/Forest Road 49A! Either something was amiss or I was now hiking through the Twilight Zone. I suddenly was not making such good time.

I started looking for a good lunch spot when, out of the corner of my eye, I saw two people walking through the woods off to my right. After a few more steps I realized that these two people were dressed exactly like Gay and Cathy. And they had with them a dog that, from a distance, looked all the world like Cali. The coincidences were astounding.

When Gay saw me, she yelled over, "I don't think you're on the trail."

I ambled over, and they were standing right next to a Kaibab Plateau/Arizona Trail sign.

Of all the indignities.

Arriving at the rendezvous point early, Gay and Cathy had decided to hike in to meet me. Only they decided to follow the trail, which, coming from the south, was well marked, if not well worn.

As we were setting up camp at the Forest Service campground near Jacob Lake, the clouds moved in and the air started to smell wet. By morning, it was deluging. We handled the downpour like experienced outdoorspeople: We quickly broke camp, drove over to the Jacob Lake Inn, and ate breakfast, hoping that the rain would abate. When it did—barely—we drove back to the trail, and Cali and I started hiking under dreary skies through

Sunrise in the Saddle Mountain Wilderness, Kaibab National Forest
❖❖❖

GAY GANGEL-FAYHEE

A reassuring trail marker, Kaibab Plateau
❖❖❖

gorgeous woods consisting of lodgepole pine, spruce, fir, and aspen. At this point we were at 8,000 feet, an altitude that feels very comfortable to me. Here the trail was, indeed, a trail—well defined, well graded, and well marked. It was wonderful. Cali had recovered from her run-in with the cactus and, with the temperature in the low forties, she bounded through the woods, happy as a pig in slop. I hiked 17 miles by 3 PM.

Gay had chosen a lovely little campsite well off the highway, but it was getting cold fast. The snow started falling before I had finished cooking dinner, and it fell most of the night. (Wasn't it just three days ago that my nose was getting sizzled under a scorching sun?) Gay was not pleased. When she signed on to help me with my logistics through this first stretch, she did so with the understanding that Arizona would live up to its warm-weather reputation. In the morning, once again, we quickly broke camp and drove to Jacob Lake for breakfast.

By the time I returned to the trail, the sun had broken out and the weather was so gorgeous that I could not resist giggling. Of all the beautiful things—both man-made and natural—that can be found on this planet, few can aesthetically touch northern Arizona on a pretty fall day. The aspen, gleaming in their golden autumnal splendor, glistened under a canopy of snow. The color of the sky approached cobalt, and the air was crisp and invigorating. I stopped for lunch next to a small lake (which actually had clean-looking water in it) that was in the middle of a huge, deep-grass meadow completely surrounded by aspen, some of which sported red leaves, some orange, some gold, some still green. Life simply could not be better at this point, unless I was on the trail with my wife. My cake was iced when I rounded a bend just before descending into yet another aspen-ringed valley, and there was Gay, who had once again hiked in to meet me. Cathy, who is an elite-class trail runner, had gone ahead to sprint a quick 2,000 kilometers before evening. Gay, Cali, and I strolled mellowly through the heart and soul of a perfect trail day.

We had planned to camp at East Rim Overlook, which offered up a heart-fluttering view of Marble Canyon and the now-distant Vermillion Cliffs; but, because I still had not procured a camping permit for the Grand Canyon, we drove directly to North Rim Village in the hope that I could arrange a way to traverse the canyon (*the* Canyon) legally. When I finished fine-tuning my trail itinerary in August, I called the Grand Canyon Powers That Be to arrange for a camping permit for Phantom Ranch, located on the mighty Colorado River at the very bottom of the canyon. They laughed at me. Come to find out that Phantom Ranch camping permits become available five months ahead of time and are snatched up five months and two seconds ahead of time. So, every single one of the permits for the night I wanted to stay at Phantom Ranch—October 9—were gone by the previous May 9. I had been told there were occasional cancellations, but to take advantage of a cancellation, I had to be at the ranger station at 8 AM on October 8. And I had to be there in person; Gay could not handle this for

> **"***Of all the beautiful things—both man-made and natural—that can be found on this planet, few can aesthetically touch northern Arizona on a pretty fall day.***"**

me. We stopped by the ranger station as soon as we arrived at the park, and I was told not to hold my breath—there probably wouldn't be a permit available for me the next day.

Despondent, I prepared myself mentally for the nearly unthinkable: a one-day, nonstop, 24-mile crossing of the Grand Canyon. Not only was I intimidated by the thought of the sheer physical exertion, but at the same

time I was bummed that I would have to hurry across and through the most
noteworthy geologic feature in the Western Hemisphere. I have hiked into
and out of the Grand Canyon twice before (including a down-and-up-in-
one-day marathon from the South Rim one intensely hot August day back
when I was younger and more stupid), but you never approach the Grand
Canyon with a been-there-done-that mentality. A person can never visit the
Grand Canyon too many times; a person can never visit it enough.

On my way out of the ranger station, the ranger yelled that perhaps
there would be a cancellation at the Phantom Ranch hotel/lodge/dormitory,
which is operated by a private concessionaire, rather than by the Park
Service. She told me that such cancellations are extremely rare, but in my
circumstance it might be worth finding out if there was one. I called the
concessionaire's headquarters in, of all places, Denver, and, sure enough,
there was a cancellation in one of the dormitories. The person on the phone
said I was an extremely lucky person. She asked if I wanted the $28 steak
dinner or the $23 stew dinner at Phantom Ranch. I opted for steak.

After an easy 17 miles from East Rim Overlook into North Rim Village
the next morning, I started focusing on the serious challenge that lay ahead.
I'm not talking about the challenge of crossing the Canyon. No, I was talking about the fact that, the next morning, Gay, Cathy, and Cali were scheduled to drive home—meaning that in three trail days I would actually have
to start lugging a full backpack. I would not see my wife for almost two
months, the longest we have ever been apart. When I hiked the 500-mile
Colorado Trail in 1991 and the 750-mile Colorado section of the Continental Divide Trail in 1995, I saw Gay almost every weekend, and that made
both of those hikes even more wonderful. There was a time when I would
have scoffed at feeling down about having the love of my life heading back
home. I would have considered myself an oversentimental wuss. But no
longer. I was going to miss my spouse bad.

As I was starting to feel preemptively lonesome, something magical
happened. Understanding that there is no such thing as a bad sunset over the
Grand Canyon, we were blessed with one for the record book. Even the employees at the North Rim were abuzz over this sunset. The sun snuck its way
beneath a bank of cirrus clouds that went from horizon to horizon. The ef-
fect was awesome. It was mesmerizing. And it lasted for more than an hour.

Sunset with the Vermillion Cliffs in the distance, Saddle Mountain Wilderness
❖.❖.❖

As darkness gathered I realized that, like few other places on earth, the Grand Canyon presents a complete sensory-overload package. It wants for nothing, and if it contained more towers, cliffs, promontories, or colorful rock striations, your eyes would have no choice but to pop straight out of your head.

At eight o'clock the next morning, we pulled into the Kaibab Trail parking lot. Gay walked down the trail with me for a few hundred yards, then she stopped, looked deeply into my eyes, and gave me the kind of full-body hug that only a wife can lay on her husband.

"Be careful, my love," was all she said before heading back up the trail.

I T WAS 14 MILES AND 6,000 vertical feet down to Phantom Ranch. If there is a more beautiful 14-mile hike on this planet, I would pay dearly to interface with it. I was walking through a superlative on a planetary scale. To top everything off, the temperature was in the mid seventies and the sky was clear.

It felt strange to suddenly be dealing with toe-scrunching downhill. Since I had hiked up the Kaibab Plateau on my first day out, the most note-worthy topographic feature I had come across was a picnic table. That's the

> **"***It was 14 miles and 6,000 vertical feet down to Phantom Ranch. If there is a more beautiful 14-mile hike on this planet, I would pay dearly to interface with it.***"**

strangest thing about this area: The only other canyon system in North America that can legitimately be uttered in the same breath as the Grand Canyon is Mexico's *Las Barrancas del Cobre*, an area I have visited more than twenty times. That complex is a system of many canyons. You are surprised, as you walk along, if you *don't* run into yet another canyon. Here at the Grand Canyon, there is only the one main canyon, and that canyon, although not the world's deepest, has a larger displacement than any other

Looking into Bright Angel Canyon from North Rim, Grand Canyon National Park
◆ ◆ ◆

canyon, gorge, or valley on earth. Below Phantom Ranch, there are still *200 miles* of canyon. Yet, the surrounding territory is as flat as a table top. There is no natural warning that the Grand Canyon is up ahead. I would love to have seen the look on Don Lopez de Cardenas' face when, after exploring hundreds of miles of relatively featureless terrain, his expedition—the first Europeans to lay eyes on this place—stumbled onto the South Rim in 1540. And I would love to have heard his report to his boss, Coronado: "Uh, chief, you ain't gonna *believe* this . . ."

After passing Roaring Springs, which is so prodigious it supplies water for both rims, the trail switchbacked its way down to Bright Angel Creek, and it basically followed that creek all the way to the Colorado River. Halfway to Phantom Ranch I stopped for a snack break in the luscious shade at Cottonwood Campground. Later I pulled over for a quarter-mile side hike to Ribbon Falls. When I'm on a long hike, I am usually very reluctant to take side hikes, even short ones, either because of fatigue, laziness, or fear of injury. (It would be the pits to twist an ankle on a side hike.) But this diversion was compelling, and to say I am glad I decided to visit Ribbon Falls is an understatement. I have never seen anything like Ribbon Falls in my life. The water fell from a lofty overhang and landed atop a silt, algae-covered hill that looked for all the world like a miniature Devil's Tower. The trail climbs up and behind the falls, so the entire east side of Bright Angel Canyon can be viewed through misty water. I could have spent the rest of my life there, happily earning a nickname like "Ribbon Falls Fayhee" or "The Old Man of the Falls," but I was equally compelled to reach Phantom Ranch at a decent hour, so I did not linger long. Three miles from the Colorado River, Bright Angel Canyon slots up tight. On this trail the month before, two hikers were swept away and killed by a flash flood. I was keeping my eyes so peeled I must have looked like one of the zombie characters from *Night of the Living Dead.*

I was passing other hikers at the rate of about a hundred a second. As a matter of fact, I was pretty stunned at the number of people on the trail—all the more so because, between the Utah border and the North Rim, I had not passed a single other hiker. But I was not bothered as badly as you might think. I am by nature a fairly gregarious person. One of the things I like most about traveling in the backcountry is spending time with the kinds

Above South Bright Angel Canyon at sunset, Grand Canyon National Park
◆ ◆ ◆

of people inclined, like me, to hoist a pack and venture away from the city lights. Hikers seem to have a common ground that transcends demographics or ideology, and I find that very refreshing in an era when it often seems like civilization is crumbling beneath our very feet.

I arrived at Phantom Ranch at two o'clock. As I was registering in the main lodge, which doubles as the facility's dining room, I noticed there was beer for sale. Very cold-looking beer, with water droplets dripping down the sides of the cans. I parked it there for an hour, basically enjoying heaven for a mere $3 a can.

AFTER DROPPING MY PACK in the small, ten-person dorm, I showered and ventured forth to explore Phantom Ranch, which, back in the early part of the century, was a working ranch before it evolved into a tourist destination. Now it is home to seventeen full-time employees whose only link to the outside world is via an ancient telephone, thrice-weekly visits by a helicopter bringing in supplies, and, of course, the hundreds of visitors that pass through it every day. When these employees, some of whom have been here as long as ten years, leave Phantom Ranch, they do so on foot.

I whiled away the rest of the afternoon reading in the sun next to the creek. Before dinner, a group of people accumulated in the gathering darkness in front of the lodge. I commented to the man sitting next to me that it looked like we were in the middle of a limpers convention. Everyone who was not sitting down was limping, and most of those who were sitting were talking about limping. Some people obviously couldn't decide which leg to limp on. I've been in physical therapy facilities located in the biggest ski county in North America that had a lower percentage of people limping. The man next to me chuckled at my observation. Soon after, he got up and limped off without saying a word. I was inwardly tickled that I was holding up so well. I couldn't have mustered a convincing limp in the middle of this crowd if I tried. Several times I got up and walked around just to show off my lack of limping.

After dinner I strolled past the campground, which was brimming with tents, to the river. I crossed the suspension bridge, the brown waters of the river churning malevolently below. I could not look down for long without feeling dizzy. On the other side, a half-dozen desert bighorns grazed on the lush riparian vegetation with impunity. By the time I returned to my dorm, it was full. I spent a sleepless night—kept awake by a veritable cacophony of snores. I would much rather have been in a tent down at the campground. The wake-up knock came at 4:30 AM, an hour that is not normally my friend. I chose to forgo breakfast at the lodge, fearing that my 9-mile, 4,500-foot ascent to the South Rim might be compromised by a full stomach. It was light enough to start hiking at 6:05 AM, and I did just that. I had been told by several people in my dorm that if I was a lot more hard core than I appeared to be, I could make it to the rim in five hours. Six or seven was more likely, they said. I took that as a challenge, deciding that I would top out by eleven o'clock, come hell or high water.

The first mile of the Bright Angel Trail parallels the river—a great warm-up. Then it hangs a hard left and begins the climb. The sky was overcast and there was an intermittent drizzle. I flew up the trail without stopping or even slowing down. I love being a strong hiker, and on this day I was deriving pure joy from the simple act of locomotion. Before I reached Indian Garden Campground—the halfway point—I started passing hikers on their way down. Shortly thereafter, a spigot of humanity was turned on. I wish I had counted the number of hikers I passed. Surely it was more than 500, and the act of having to step off the trail to let others pass every 0.2 nanosecond was slowing me down. Still, at nine o'clock I was 1.8 miles from the rim. I made it there at 10:03—less than four hours after leaving Phantom Ranch.

As I turned to take in the view of the canyon I had just crossed, I looked around and noticed that everyone around me was bundled up. By the time I caught my breath, I realized it was damned cold. A touch of winter was in the air. Still, I was on cloud nine. I was feeling wonderful. My first stretch was over, and the beginning of my AZT experience was suddenly a thing of the past. I caught a shuttle bus to where my truck was parked and patted myself on the back.

Then a sad realization hit: 96 miles down, only 650 left to go.

South Rim *of the* Grand Canyon *to* Flagstaff

◆·◆·◆·◆·◆·◆·◆·◆·◆·◆·◆

S OMETIMES THE LAW OF INERTIA works for you and sometimes it does not. If I had let myself rest for even one instant after arriving at South Rim Village, I likely would have remained happily and comfortably at rest for the remainder of the day. One of the most important rules of successful long-distance backpacking is taking aggressive advantage of every opportunity to park your posterior. In my excitement to arrange my logistics for the five-day, 85-mile haul from the South Rim to Flagstaff, I forgot—or at least disregarded—that rule. Rather than catch my breath for a few hours, I remained in motion. I almost sprinted from the trailhead at the South Rim to my truck, which I had left in a public lot adjacent to the park's backcountry office.

After a delightfully prodigious and greasy breakfast at a near-at-hand cafeteria in South Rim Village, I drove directly to the park's laundromat/public shower facility. Even though I had power-showered the day before down at Phantom Ranch, I could not pass up a chance to scrub and preen once again. More than anything, I miss hot showers when I'm out in the woods, and I rarely pass up a chance to shower or bathe when I come off the trail and return to civilization.

While the washers and dryers magically turned my hiking clothes from disgusting items that ought to be thrown away (if not burned) into things that can be worn without eliciting gags from any goats I might happen by, I dashed out to my truck to organize my supply boxes. Since this was to be my test section for my food-and-water-cache strategy, I was extremely anxious. Even though I had been roused from the Land of Nod at the ungodly hour of 4:30 AM down at Phantom Ranch, and

even though I had just hiked from the very bottom of the Grand Canyon to the very top without hardly slowing down, I could not make myself relax. The motion half of the Law of Inertia had me in its clutches and it would not let me go.

I drove to Russell Tank, where I planned to stash my first cache. After hiding my food and water containers behind a felled tree, I piled loose brush atop the cache, took a GPS bearing, and walked away, hoping for the best. I then proceeded toward faraway Lockwood Tank, where I planned to hide my second supply cache. By the time I arrived there, I had driven almost 50 miles on rugged dirt road since leaving the South Rim, and it was getting dark fast. It was time to stop for the day. Even though the area around the rancid-looking tank was muddy and overflowing with evidence of recent mass bovine visitation, I simply could go no farther. My eyelids were getting heavier by the minute. I opted to make camp right next to my truck. Before setting up my tent I started heating a 12-gallon can of extra-spicy chili. Just as I was about to enjoy the first tantalizing bite, I heard some precipitation start pitter-pattering on the top of my camper. Since I had parked my truck's bow into the wind, I had not seen the storm front approaching. I walked around the truck and dropped my spoon. It looked like a horizon-to-horizon malevolent gray wave was about to break directly over me.

I ran as fast as I could up a nearby hill with a water container and placed it behind a juniper with zero in the way of additional camouflage. I

◆·◆·◆

Summer ground cover near Grandview Point, South Rim of the Grand Canyon

Ponderosa pine near Grandview Point, with the Grand Canyon in the distance
◆◆◆

blew off setting out a food cache, meaning I would have to carry some extra chow and fuel for the first few days of the next stretch. I didn't even take the time to punch in a GPS coordinate, figuring that, if I could not find Lockwood Tank, I ought not to be out here on the AZT.

Barely taking time to secure my stove and chili, I hopped into the driver's seat and began an all-out effort to make it to the closest paved road before I got snowed in. Within minutes, the snow was falling in big flakes so heavily, I could barely see. I was less worried about accumulation than I was about the red clay-looking roads becoming saturated and, thus, impassable. I've burned a clutch out of a vehicle while trying to make my way along a muddy, middle-of-nowhere red-clay road, and I did not relish the thought of a repeat performance.

It was a tense drive out, and that tension was exacerbated by the fact that driving with headlights on during a snowstorm is hypnotic. I was so sleepy it seemed like I was on the verge of hallucination territory. At one point a herd of more than fifty elk ran across the dirt road in front of me, seemingly in slow motion. It was some minutes later before I began to wonder if I had actually seen those elk or if my sleep-starved imagination was playing tricks on me.

It took two hours to reach the town of Tusayan. I was so exhausted I decided to splurge on a motel room; but, because of the nasty weather, every room in town was taken. I ended up driving back near Russell Tank— where this ordeal had begun almost nine hours earlier. I set up my tent and decided to sleep until 8:30 the next morning.

Which I did, happily.

BY LATE AFTERNOON I had placed my last supply cache for the South Rim-to-Flagstaff stretch at Abineau Trailhead, on the northern side of the massive San Francisco Peaks—Arizona's tallest mountains. I drove back to South Rim and got a campsite. After the sun rose the next morning I tried to pick up my monster Gregory Robson internal-frame pack, which was filled to brimming. I figured that I must have been standing on a strap or something, because it simply would not budge. To my dismay and consternation, I was standing on no strap that I could see. My pack, alas, weighed at least 300 pounds. I opened it up, jumped head first into the main compartment, and began tossing out items like a dog tosses dirt out of a hole. Out came the heavier and more comfortable Bibler Eldorado tent; in went the lighter and less comfortable Sierra Designs Flash Magic. Out came the extra jacket and the twelve emergency Snickers bars. By the time I finished, my pack was down to 200 pounds—and I could still barely get it off the ground. I was distraught.

I took a taxi from the South Rim out to the trailhead at Grandview Firetower, once again leaving my truck near the park's backcountry office. It was 12 level miles to Russell Tank. In my memory, those 12 miles are a blur of pain and disorientation caused by pack-weight-borne fatigue. I remember pretty, sun-dappled pine woods and several splendid views down toward the faraway Diné Nation to the east. I lurched along what ended up being a very well-designed and implemented section of ridiculously mellow trail, yet the only thing on which I could focus was getting to camp so I could remove the torturous device that I had voluntarily placed upon my innocent back. I was having trouble negotiating even modest trail meanderings. My legs would try their darndest to follow a curve, but my pack seemed to have a mind all its own; it wanted to go straight no matter what direction the trail took. Not for the first time in my life I started asking myself, as I staggered along the trail, why on earth do I subject myself to such discomfort and indignity?

Still, I made it to Russell Tank in slightly less than four hours.

I decided to leave some of my gear and clothing behind in my food box. Even though I managed to pull out several pounds worth of seemingly extraneous items, I could not fathom why my pack was feeling so heavy. I was carrying little in the way of extra food, and had only a half bottle of fuel. I had no water filter, and neither was I overly encumbered by extra cigars. Then it dawned on me: I was being a lightweight! I had been so spoiled by having Gay along during the Utah-to-South Rim stretch that I forgot what it was like to carry a full pack. I decided right then and there to suck it up and

Indian paintbrush, Kaibab National Forest, south of the Grand Canyon
❖❖❖

start hiking like the bad hombre I pretend, sometimes, to think I am. Still, I felt it could not hurt to leave a few items behind in my food box—out of principle, if nothing else.

I set up my tent in the middle of a well-used hunters' camp. Since my water container held 6 gallons, I could enjoy a thorough wash. There are definitely two kinds of trail days: those that end with a bath and those that do not. I had opted for larger water containers with this in mind.

When I had placed my cache here at Russell Tank, there was a family of hunters camped at the very site where my tent now sat. They were very nice people, and we chatted for ten or fifteen minutes. Better stated, they chatted. And what they chatted about was bears. I was told in no uncertain terms that this place was Bear Central.

No sooner had I changed into clean clothes than I began fretting big time about bears. In a life spent camping in bear country, I count myself fortunate in that I have laid eyes on several ursines, but I have never been involved in an "incident." I have never been attacked and I have never had my camp pillaged. But good luck is a fickle companion; it can run out on you at any moment. I decided to deal with my bear concern by gathering several dozen cords of firewood and building a blaze as large as a medium-size house—although I've always wondered, perhaps, if campfires don't serve as beacons for bears, rather than deterrents. Like maybe the bear would have never known I was here, except that he saw my fire blazing away.

It is very rare for me to build fires when I'm on the trail. I reluctantly buy into the idea that fires are antithetical to the pro-environment stance in which I believe and espouse. Fires use fuel that is best left for soil regeneration purposes. They create unsightly and destructive fire rings, and they make you smell like smoke. Since there was abundant juniper wood lying around, an existing fire ring and, as far as my imagination could tell, at least fifty bears drawing up plans at that very moment to attack my camp, I threw

Agave, South Rim of the Grand Canyon
◆.◆.◆

my environmental concerns right out the window. I had a fairly substantial conflagration going well before dark.

It was exceedingly pleasant to sit next to a campfire. Like most out-doorspeople "mature" enough to remember the "good ol' days"—when Kelty packs reigned supreme and when no backpacker would be caught dead without his or her Sierra Cup—I find myself missing fires, which were as much a part of the camping landscape as sagging A-frame tents and scratchy wool hats until about the late 1970s, when people began realizing the dam-age their campfires were doing to the environment.

> **"***I decided to deal with my bear concern by gathering several dozen cords of firewood and building a blaze as large as a medium-size house—although I've always wondered, perhaps, if campfires don't serve as beacons for bears, rather than deterrents.***"**

While sitting next to my fire near Russell Tank, I made a decision that seemed to be profound at the time: I decided to build campfires as often as my conscience would allow while on the AZT. I convinced myself that the biosphere likely would not collapse as a result of a solitary hiker building occasional campfires while on a two-month hike through the middle of a state that seemed to boast abundant firewood.

I became excited at the thought of spending my evenings on the AZT sitting before a dancing set of flames, sipping tea, and jotting down Deep Thoughts in my journal as fast as my pen could move. But this mental momentum did not make it even one step past Russell Tank. I built nary another fire on my trek to Mexico. My passion for fire has been doused by habit in the past twenty years, I guess. Sigh. I certainly did enjoy that one fire that night, though.

I tossed several logs on the fire before retiring, hoping that the flames would keep the local bears at bay. I expected to sleep with one eye open, lest

*Aspen modeling autumn's touch, with the
snow-covered San Francisco Peaks in the distance*
◆◆◆

Ancient bristlecone pine, San Francisco Peaks, 11,500 feet elevation
◆◆◆

any large four-legged creatures came creeping into camp bent on heisting my food. I fell asleep almost immediately, which is a rarity in my insomnia-afflicted life. I slept the night through, and if any bears visited my camp, they were courteous enough to go about their business quietly.

After hiding my water and food containers, I hit the trail by 7:30 the next morning. The air was crisp and the sky was cloudless. My pack felt much lighter, even though I knew, in actuality, it was not. By realizing that I was being a wuss the day before, I started focusing more on the cranial aspect of this hike. I'm not able to hike the distances or the speeds I could twenty years ago, but I am a lot more focused and disciplined than I used to be. *No more whining*, I admonished myself. *Time to get strong, mentally.*

Again, the trail was beautiful and easy. It wound into and out of the juniper woods, which were getting thinner with each mile. Fifty miles ahead loomed the snow-covered San Francisco Peaks. As much as I love juniper-piñon woods and the desert environment, I am most at home in and around high mountains. The peaks seemed to beckon and spur me on. I was hiking strong and with joy in my heart.

It was only 12 miles to Lockwood Tank, and I made it there in less than four hours. I felt so good, I would have liked to have hiked several more miles, but this was where my water cache was located, so this was where I had to camp. I found a suitable campsite atop a small ridge that afforded splendid views in all directions. I spent a tranquil afternoon reading, writing, smoking, and napping. I felt more relaxed than I had at any point on this hike so far. I was finally shedding the pressure brought about by two years of planning my AZT adventure. It's not that my life back in civilization is overly complex or tense, but it is complex and tense enough. Things were working out well for me on the AZT, and now I told myself that all I had to do was get up in the morning, hike, set up camp, sleep, get up in the morning, and hike. The simplicity of long-distance hiking has always appealed to me. It's a back-to-basics existence at its most fundamental level.

As I started to prepare dinner, I came to a startling realization. In my effort to lighten my load back at Russell Tank, my spice and condiment bag had not made it back into my pack. I always carry with me soy sauce, bacon bits, parmesan cheese, curry, olive oil, garlic powder, bullion, and oregano. With those items, I figure I can make a tasty meal out of dirt and grass if

View of Cinder Hills from San Francisco Peaks, Coconino National Forest

♦ ♦ ♦

*Autumn's colors set off by an early snowfall, upper Harte Prairie,
San Francisco Peaks*

♦♦♦

necessary. My menu this fine night was to be angel hair pasta with olive oil, parmesan cheese, oregano, and garlic—one of my very favorite backcountry meals, I might add. Distraught, I found myself staring down at a bowl of pasta adorned with a provocative sauce that consisted of nothing more than air. It was a tough meal to get down, but get it down I did. When you're carrying a pack up and down mountains all day, you have to stoke the furnace.

> "*. . . the trail was beautiful and easy. It wound into and out of the juniper woods, which were getting thinner with each mile. Fifty miles ahead loomed the snow-covered San Francisco Peaks.*"

I thought about my other meals between here and Flagstaff. I had a couple of packages of Ramen, which contain their own spice packets, scheduled for the next night, so that would be OK, but at Abineau Trailhead, my last night before Flagstaff, I was to have curried beef and rice—now without the curry.

THE NEXT MORNING, the trail soon left Kaibab National Forest land and made its way along well-marked dirt roads through a checkerboard of land that was variously privately and state owned. Babbitt Ranches, which holds leases on the land hereabouts that it does not own outright, has enthusiastically embraced having the AZT cross its territory. I had spoken with the ranch foreman before starting my hike and he invited me to camp near Cedar Ranch, where, I was told, there was a reliable water source. Therefore I did not have a cache for this day's hike. It was 16 miles to Cedar Ranch, and the primitive roads the AZT followed were mostly level and in fairly good condition. The tree cover was scarce and the views were endless. The San Francisco Peaks were getting larger with each step. They covered a significant percentage of the southern horizon. I would be hiking up the side of those peaks two days hence.

The hike to Cedar Ranch was Zen-like. It was so benign that I could let my mind wander, which is always pleasant. There are two types of hiking:

one that is mellow enough to allow for daydreaming and one that is not. I passed through herds of cows, alongside small hills, and under several huge power transmission lines, all the while thinking about nothing in particular. Until, that is, it dawned on me that I had not seen an AZT marker in quite some time. This area was crisscrossed by roads, and I could have easily wandered by a trail junction. As I hiked on, I started to get worried. According to my maps, I was supposed, eventually, to descend a steep hill into a ranch camp named, poetically enough, "Tub." I walked and walked, getting more apprehensive with each step. No steep hill; no Tub. For the past three days, the trail had been well marked with AZT logo-adorned posts that were about knee high. It seemed improbable that the marking of this trail would simply end. Just as I was about to turn around despondently to go post hunting, I rounded a bend and there was the steep hill. I could easily make out a ranch house several hundred feet below me.

When I bottomed out, I saw a couple of AZT posts that had been uprooted and were lying on the side of the road. Before I knew it, I was standing directly in front of the house, and it dawned on me too late that I was committing a manners transgression of near-monumental proportions. There were two young children playing in the yard, and when they saw my disheveled, ill-groomed self walk up, they shrieked and ran into the house. Their mom soon came out and gave me a serious case of stink eye.

"Is this the Arizona Trail?" I asked limply.

"Yesss . . . ," the women very cautiously and nervously replied.

I laid a rapid-fire Cliff Notes version of my life history on her, told her what I was doing standing there in her front yard, begged forgiveness for being such an idiot, and prepared to say adios. By the time I had finished with my spiel, the woman had obviously made the decision that I was not an ax murderer disguised as a backpacker, or if I was, she could probably whup me.

It ended up that she had only been living at Tub for two months, and her husband, who worked for Babbitt Ranches, was gone for a couple of days, riding the range or getting some little doggies along or something cowboylike. I did not blame her for being apprehensive about my presence. She asked if I had enough water, and I was happy to have her fill up my water bottles. When I told her where I planned on camping that night, she got

Aspen near Harte Prairie
◆.◆.◆

visibly concerned. She told me that a friend of hers was living at Cedar Ranch, and that she would be "freaked out" if I walked up unannounced. She said her friend had only been living at Cedar Ranch for three weeks and that her husband, too, was out riding the range for a few days.

The woman at Tub suggested that she drive me the 4 miles to Cedar Ranch so that proper introductions could be made. She fired up her pickup truck and chauffeured me down the long, dusty road to Cedar Ranch.

The woman at Cedar Ranch had never heard of the AZT, even though it passes within 100 yards of her residence, and she had absolutely no idea where the water source I had been told about could be found. Since I had my bottles filled at Tub, I bade the ladies adieu and went off in search of the water I was sure was nearby. I found a decent-looking campsite, dropped my pack, and took off with my 3-gallon water bag in hand.

An hour later, I still had not found any water. Very reluctantly I returned to the ranch house. Even though I could hear the woman moving

Aspen leaves,
Coconino National Forest

◆◆◆

> **"***The simplicity of long-distance hiking has always appealed to me. It's a back-to-basics existence at its most fundamental level.***"**

around inside, she did not answer my knocks. I knew that my rudeness was approaching the point where it knew no bounds, but I needed water. So I pounded on the door. A few minutes later it opened about a half inch. I explained my plight and the woman reached her hand meekly through the crack in the door. She took my water bag and filled it. When she returned, she came out onto the porch and we chatted for a few minutes. It seemed that her loneliness had overcome her justifiable trepidation.

After setting up my tent and washing up, I looked for a safe spot on which to set my camp chair. There was prickly pear everywhere, and since my chair is filled with an inflatable air mattress/sleeping pad, I wanted to be extra careful. This was serious desert country and I was trying hard to deal with the fact that, when you get right down to it, I am intimidated by serious desert country. I love the desert on just about every aesthetic level I can think of, but I still find it intimidating. As the late Edward Abbey so often stated, it seems that every organic thing in the desert either stings, pricks, or bites. Still, the beauty of the desert overcomes, or at least mitigates, the harsher aspects of this biome.

Shortly after lighting up my evening cigar, the meanest-looking wasp I have ever seen started buzzing around camp. It hovered directly in front of my nose, then went over to investigate my pack and tent, then came back to hover once again directly in front of my nose. This went on for a half hour and, frankly, I was getting a tad tired of this insect's obtrusive presence. I don't like killing things—even things that, like this wasp, deserve to be killed. The exception, of course, is mosquitoes. The only kind of mosquito I like is a smooshed one. But that's different, because mosquitoes are designed to pester and bite. A wasp only stings when circumstances call for it.

Yet, I have no earthly idea what this wasp is up to. For all I know, it is searching out a site for a new hive, and at any moment it is going to return to its chums and beckon them to my camp. I decide that, my aversion to killing innocent creatures aside, if this wasp hovers in front of my nose one more time, I'll whack it with a magazine then stomp on it. Waspocide in the name of inner peace and tranquillity is probably all right.

In the east, the blood-red full moon rose huge. I can't remember ever seeing such a monster moon. It was the size of a pizza pan, and was so large that it looked like I could hike over to it before I went to bed. I could make out topographic features on the lunar surface with my naked eye.

It's warm enough that I stay up late—until well past seven. Just as I start to get out of my chair, the wasp comes back. It lands right on my cheek, and, in the frantic tizzy that follows, it somehow manages to get stuck in my hair. I am presented with a quandary here: splat the wasp and have wasp splat stuck in my hair or sit here and let the beast, which I'm certain is now in a foul mood, extricate itself from my locks. I end up shaking my head violently back and forth, the wasp gets dislodged, and it goes upon its merry way.

THE NEXT MORNING I discover that the trail follows dirt roads into the Coconino National Forest. By the time I top out on a parched ridge, the temperature is in the low nineties, and the bandanna that I have wrapped around my head is drenched. I'm getting tired of walking on dirt roads, even though these are very primitive and not often used. Psychologically, hiking is harder on roads than on trails, and I'm not certain why. Dirt roads are also tougher on the feet, as the roads tend to be very compact and hard.

A Forest Service person had warned me that I would have to connect a series of unmarked gravel roads about 5 miles before Abineau Trailhead. The AZT's corridor had not yet been determined in this neck of the woods, so I found myself zigzagging my way toward my water cache on roads that were flat out killing my tootsies. These roads made their way through an area that, several years earlier, had been toasted by one of the largest forest fires in Arizona history. The smell of smoke and burned wood permeated the air. The blackened tree trunks stood in stark contrast to the huge stands of aspen, which were in the height of their fall color.

Finally, I could handle walking on roads no more. I pulled out my GPS, took a bearing on Abineau Trailhead and started out cross-country. Almost immediately I was pleased to have made that decision. In an hour of hiking through the roadless woods I saw four herds of elk and three herds of deer. I walked through stands of wildflowers, and the pungent smell of autumn was pervasive and almost intoxicating. It is almost axiomatic in late-twentieth-century America: Leave the road and good things will happen.

At Abineau Trailhead I ran into a couple of old-timers who had been out on a dayhike. When I told them I was camping right up the hill, they glanced nervously at each other.

Aspen forest with undergrowth showing a touch of fall color, San Francisco Peaks
❖.❖.❖

View of San Francisco Peaks beyond a massive
field of wildflowers
◆◆◆

"You had better keep your eyes peeled for bears," one of them said as the other nodded enthusiastically.

I told them they could count on it.

Since my campsite was at 8,000 feet, it got cold fast after the sun set. I enjoyed my meal of curryless curried beef and rice, and hit the sack by seven. I don't know why, but I started feeling a little lonely. People ask me all the time about hiking solo, and I honestly answer that I have no problem whatsoever with being by myself in the woods. I know it would be safer to hike with a partner, but life is a lot simpler when you don't have to worry about other people's comfort and happiness.

While on the AZT, though, I was able to sort of cheat on the loneliness front. A buddy of mine who owns a cellular telephone company had offered me free use of one of his phones. I scoffed at first, much the same way that I scoffed when I was offered my GPS. I muttered something about the contamination of the pure wilderness experience and politely declined the offer. When I mentioned this to my wife, I could tell by the look on her face that, like it or not, I was going to be carrying a cell phone with me on the AZT.

> **"***In an hour of hiking through the roadless woods . . . I walked through stands of wildflowers, and the pungent smell of autumn was pervasive and almost intoxicating.***"**

Gay would not have been so adamant about this if we had had to pay for the phone, but once she heard the word "gratis" attached to this offer, I did not even bother to argue.

While camping there at Abineau, I did something that I swore before leaving Utah I would not do: make a gratuitous phone call from the back-country. I dialed my home phone number—just to see if the cell phone was functional, you understand.

Gay answered almost immediately. She said she had a feeling I would call that night. We chatted for only a few minutes, but it was wonderful to hear her voice, to hear her say how much she missed and loved me, and to tell me for the millionth time since we hooked up so many years ago to "be careful." I slept peacefully.

It was 25°F the next morning but I was up and on the trail before the sun came up. It was 21 miles, plus or minus, to Flagstaff and I wanted to get there as quickly as possible. My longtime friend Fosco Spinedi was scheduled to fly in from his home in Switzerland to join me for three weeks on the trail. Even though we had plans to meet that were detailed enough to make even a Swiss man happy, I still wanted to arrive early enough to deal with whatever mix-ups might occur.

The trail—yes, there was actual trail—followed a small, shady drainage for two miles into the Kachina Peaks Wilderness. It was icy and steep, and I spent a lot of time slipping and sliding. After 2,000 vertical feet of ascent, the trail left the wilderness and hooked into a primitive road that followed the entire eastern side of the mountain range. This road serves as a temporary route for the AZT. The Forest Service is trying to figure out an environmentally and culturally sensitive (these mountains are considered sacred to the Hopi Nation) way to get the trail to pass through the heart of Kachina Peaks Wilderness. But, until they do, the trail is this road, which is closed to vehicular traffic.

Although the surface was soft, and downhill all the way, and although the views were consistently stupendous, this road simply would not end. It wandered into and out of every dimple and drainage the east side of the San Francisco Peaks had to offer. By early afternoon I was convinced that I had hiked all the way around the entire mountain range. I was getting so tired that I ended up stumbling over my own feet on several occasions.

By the time I became convinced that I was no longer on the AZT, but rather in some sort of hikers' purgatory, I arrived at Shultz Pass Road on the outskirts of Flagstaff. Instead of dealing with the vagaries of hitchhiking into town, I pulled out my trusty cell phone and called a taxi.

Thirty minutes later I hooked up with Fosco at our prearranged meeting point. As I fell onto the bed in my hotel room, it dawned on me: 180 miles down, only 570 to go.

Flagstaff *to* Pine

◆·◆·◆·◆·◆·◆·◆·◆·◆·◆·◆·◆

THE DAY BEFORE RECONNECTING with the AZT, Fosco Spinedi, a meteorologist with the Swiss National Weather Service, and I were sitting in a bar in downtown Flagstaff shooting the breeze and talking trail skinny. The bartender overheard the conversation and made a few queries. I told him I was hiking the AZT from Utah to Mexico and would, in the morning, start the seven-day, 101-mile segment from Flagstaff to Pine.

"Better keep your eyes peeled for tarantulas," he admonished. "Where you'll be hiking for the next few days, there's lots of 'em. Lots."

I just shook my head and smiled, thinking that there must be some sort of conspiracy/joke among Arizona residents to get me to "keep my eyes peeled" for *something* every millimeter of the way. First it was flash floods between the Utah border and the Grand Canyon, then it was bears—not once, but twice—between the South Rim and Flagstaff.

Now, it was *tarantulas*, of all things.

I have, over the years, come across more than a few tarantulas. I even had one jump onto the side of my neck while I was relaxing next to a river down in Mexico. (Now *that* was an invigorating few seconds.) I am well enough acquainted with various members of the Theraphosidae family to know that, first, they are highly overrated as things to fear and, second, they are low-desert-dwelling arachnids. For the first six days of the next leg—between Flagstaff and the Mogollon Rim—the trail traverses territory with an average elevation well above 6,000 feet. With

nighttime temperatures getting downright frosty, I told Fosco that we need not fret over tarantulas, and that the bartender obviously did not know a tarantula from a mai tai. Fosco wanted to know if we needed to keep our eyes peeled for mai tais. I told him, unfortunately no.

We caught a ride with a Forest Service employee back out to the trail. The AZT route through Flagstaff was not totally established, so we were dropped off at Sandy's Canyon Trail, a brand-new, mile-long spur that intersected the AZT just south of Fisher's Point.

It was weird suddenly to be hiking with a partner. Even though Gay and Cathy were with me between Utah and the North Rim, they did not spend all that much time actually *with* me on the trail. Fosco was slated to be with me for almost three weeks and 200-plus miles. By the time he leaves the trail at Roosevelt Lake to go home, this hike will be almost as much his as it is mine.

I have known Fosco, who lives in Ticino, the Italian-speaking part of Switzerland, since 1973, when he was an exchange student at the high school I attended in eastern Virginia. In the past twenty-three years he has visited me several times; but, even though we have long talked about doing a backpacking trip, this will mark the first time we have ever hit the trail together. I am a little nervous about it. I have witnessed firsthand how close friendships can deteriorate under the social magnifying glass of trail life.

I impress Fosco immediately by losing the trail almost within sight of the parking lot where we were dropped off. Even though we were told specifically that we would need to follow Sandy's Canyon Trail for 1 mile

◆·◆·◆

Sunset over Mormon Lake with Mormon Mountain in the distance

before intersecting the AZT, after ten minutes of failing to see a sign, I panic, spy what in retrospect was probably an old deer trail heading off in the basic direction we needed to go, and proclaim in no uncertain terms that it "must be the AZT."

Fosco looks less than convinced. Smart man. Coming as he does from a place where backcountry trails are extremely well used and obvious, he thinks I surely must be mistaken, but is gracious enough to follow my lead without too much dissension.

We bushwhack through the thick deciduous woods for a half hour, following the lower reaches of picturesque, sandstone cliff-lined Walnut Canyon, which is maybe 100 feet deep. Finally, after climbing out of the canyon, we stumble upon the AZT. I smile smugly and tell Fosco that I knew where we were going the whole time. The look on his face says something like: *I can't believe I'm following this moron through the heart of Arizona. I'm dead meat!*

We plan to hike only 10 miles today, to Lakeview Campground, where we have placed a supply cache. We follow new trail through the forest for 5 miles before reaching Marshall Lake. Ever since the snowstorm that chased me out of Lockwood Tank, the weather has been perfect, with clear skies, and temperatures in the mid sixties to low seventies during the day and in the mid twenties to mid thirties at night. Now, however, the wind is picking up and banks of malevolent-looking clouds are moving in slowly.

We were told that the trail disappears at Marshall Lake and that we would have to travel cross-country along the lip of a modest mesa that parallels the highway connecting Flagstaff with Pine. But the trail did *not* disappear. Quite the contrary. Just past Marshall Lake there was a trailhead sign, and although the quality of the tread diminished somewhat, it made for pleasant walking.

It begins to drizzle. Instantly, the trail becomes a quagmire of clay. Tons of dirt with the consistency of Super Glue clings to our soles. We increase in height by several inches per step, with a disproportionate per-

The author's hiking companion, Fosco Spinedi, celebrates water on Verde River
◆◆◆

M. JOHN FAYHEE

centage of the mud sticking stubbornly to our heels. So, not only are we getting taller as we go along—sort of like backpacking in platform boots—but, concurrently, we are leaning farther and farther forward, as though our platform hiking boots have high heels. Then we get to a point where the mud on one boot detaches itself in a single fell clump, so, without warning, one leg is 5 inches shorter than the other. We slip, slide, and stagger our way down the trail for several hours. Anyone looking at us from a distance would swear we were drunk.

The most noteworthy aspect of this comedy of perambulative errors stems from the fact that the trail is covered with tarantulas. We could not believe our eyes, which we were very definitely keeping peeled. It was like some sort of Tarantula Exodus was transpiring. It couldn't have been a more orderly migration had a tarantula Moses been ahead of the pack, waving a staff and admonishing his minions to keep the faith. And this after I told Fosco there was no way in the world we would see any tarantulas in these parts.

> **"***The most noteworthy aspect of this comedy of perambulative errors stems from the fact that the trail is covered with tarantulas. . . . It was like some sort of Tarantula Exodus was transpiring.***"**

Moreover, these tarantulas were aggressive. If we stepped too close, they would come charging toward us with fire in their eyes, like eight-legged wolverines. One even jumped on top of my boot and tried to wrestle me to the ground.

By mid afternoon, I took a GPS bearing on our supply cache and we descended from the mesa down to Lakeview Campground. Fosco was dog

Unnamed creek south of Mormon Lake with San Francisco Peaks in the distance

◆◆◆

tired and fairly depressed at the climatological circumstances. Fosco is a man who, in his own opinion, brings bad weather with him wherever he goes, which is sort of a funny thought for a meteorologist. He felt certain that if there was any place on earth where he could safely expect to revel in sunshine and warmth, it would be Arizona. Instead, the clouds began to look more ominous, the rain began to fall harder, and we began to hear thunder in the distance. This would not be so bad except that Fosco's tent is not exactly the latest in modern, high-tech backpacking design and technology. Actually, he bought it from J.C. Penney for $25 in 1978. He told me that even when it was brand new, when it came to protection from precipitation, he might as well sleep in a swimming pool.

I invite Fosco to share my diminutive tent, and am glad when he refuses. My Sierra Designs Flash Magic, an inexpensive single-wall tent made of nonbreatheable fabric, was advertised as a two-person shelter, but experience has shown me that if two people share it, they had better be on fairly intimate terms. It is tiny. And Fosco snores. Bad. I would much rather Fosco be miserable and wet by himself than for him to be dry, cozy, and sawing 150-decibel logs 6 inches from my face.

Fosco is not in the best of spirits. Not only has the weather got him down, but he has the makings of what appears to be a fairly nasty blister. While I am wearing lightweight Vasque Clarions, Fosco is wearing heavy leather mountaineering boots. I told him back in Flagstaff that I deemed it unlikely we would be encountering any glaciers, but he was adamant about sticking with his original footwear plan, even though he was also carrying a soft pair of ankle-high Nikes that, in my opinion, were much better suited to the AZT than his heavy boots.

With a dank chill in the air, we both retire before sunset. I cannot help but notice that I am hitting the hay earlier and earlier every night. Before this journey is over, it will be getting dark by six, and I will be enduring or enjoying—depending on my disposition *du jour*—more than twelve hours a day in my teensy tent. When I'm back in civilization, I sometimes fantasize about tent marathons, but when I'm out in the woods, I can get to the point where I feel like yelling "No *mas!*" after enjoying an entire night's worth of snooze time, only to look at my watch and realize it's just 1 AM. When it's cold and drizzly, however, I have no compunction about crawling into my

3-pound trail abode as soon as the dishes are done and my post-dinner cigar is savored.

I tell Fosco to sleep tight and don't let the tarantulas bite. He smiles, but there is little mirth behind his facial expression. We are fortunate, as it does little more than sprinkle off and on during the night; but, by morning, the clouds are still with us. Our gear is wet, which makes packing up less than joyous.

I cannot believe how quickly Fosco gets ready. As soon as he hears me fire up the stove, he bounds out of the rack, runs over, consumes two sips of some stinky herbal tea, shovels three bites of granola into his mouth, runs off still chewing the granola, takes his tent down and returns with his pack on his back, ready to move out. It has been about 15 seconds since he egressed his tent. I, on the other hand, am just starting to boil water for my second cup of coffee.

Although I will try to speed things up in the morning while Fosco is with me, he will have to get used to my deliberate pace in the morning. I am a ritual-oriented person when I am on a long hike. I have my evening rituals—washing up, having a cup of tea at four o'clock, and smoking a cigar after dinner—and I have my morning rituals: washing my face with a warm washcloth, having two cups of coffee, and eating a hot breakfast. This is just the way it is.

We climb back onto the mesa and begin our muddy slog to Pine Grove Campground, where we will eat lunch and where the AZT, we are told, flat out ends. Because of the mud, we are moving slowly, and, once again, we are joined by hordes of tarantulas.

In every direction, the thick, viscous cloud cover is down at eye level. It's like heavy liquid swishing slowly over the landscape. It takes two dreary hours to reach the paved road going up to Ashhurst Lake. I never thought I would be ecstatic at the thought of hiking 2 miles on pavement, but after dealing with all that mud for the past 7 or 8 miles, this feels like liberation. And here the tarantulas disappear. I see only a handful more all the way to Mexico.

According to the information we gleaned from the Forest Service back in Flagstaff, we need to begin a cross-country segment at Pine Grove. While Fosco rests at a picnic table, I go off in search of the red surveyor's flagging that we were told marks the route that the AZT will one day follow. I was

View from Highview Point, Mogollon Rim
◆.◆.◆

unsuccessful in finding it, but that didn't bother me too much, as I knew all we had to do was walk southwest and, in less than a mile, we would come across an old railroad bed that we could follow pretty much all the way to Dairy Springs Campground, which, according to my GPS, was only about 5 miles away as the crow flies.

We took a compass bearing and began walking through woods that, on a sunny day, would have been bright and cheery. With the repressive cloud cover still dominating the entire sky, it made for depressing, sniffle-nosed going. The knee-high grass was wet, and soon my boots and socks were soaked through—the downside of wearing light, permeable footwear.

"*In every direction, the thick, viscous cloud cover is down at eye level. It's like heavy liquid swishing slowly across the landscape.*"

Finally we began to see occasional red flags, and they led us right to the long-abandoned railroad bed. We had thought our route would, from then on, be smooth and grassy. *Ix-nay.* This railroad bed consisted of nothing more than the exposed, loose bowling ball-size rocks on which the long-gone tracks were once laid. It made for deliberate going. At frequent intervals the surveyors' flags deviated from the railroad bed, heading off at varying angles into the forest. We could not decide whether it was better to follow the flags, which, with the trail as yet unbuilt, seemed to travel willy-nilly through the woods, or stick with the railroad bed, which was clearly designed by mean-spirited people who, more than anything, hated the notion of anyone being able to walk along their creation with any degree of comfort.

We ended up mixing the two strategies, following the flags until they led to woods too thick to traverse, then returning to the railroad bed until our feet got too sore to continue. At one point we came across a large pile of rusty railroad spikes. Fosco picked up a few to take back to Switzerland as souvenirs, but I decided that I could use a couple dozen of them for decorative purposes back at my casa. According to my GPS, we were only a couple

Highview Point overlook, Coconino National Forest
◆·◆·◆

View from near Highview Point, Mogollon Rim

◆◆◆

miles from Dairy Springs, where we planned to camp for the night, so I crammed as many spikes as I could into my Robson. By the time I finished, I needed help donning my pack, but I figured I could carry 20 or so extra pounds of iron as far as Dairy Springs, where I would leave the spikes in my food cache box. Little did I know that, by merely thinking that thought, I had laid a whammy on poor, innocent Fosco and, more important, on myself.

Soon thereafter, the surveyor's flagging ceased and desisted, and we could stomach the notion of following the rough rail bed no longer. So, we decided to seek out a power line that was marked on our forest map. That decision was not exactly Einsteinian. The power lines followed a series of steep up-and-downs and, on those rare occasions when the lines did not go through woods so dense we could scarcely move between the trees, they passed through waist-high, thorny brush that was obviously genetically designed by some very mad scientists to serve as a physical impediment to any sort of animal larger than bacteria. Finally we gave up and made our way out to the highway. The entire time we had been experiencing our misery-fest along the power lines, Fosco kept muttering that there was something directionally amiss. And he was right. I was of the opinion that we were heading pretty much due south and getting close to Dairy Springs, but it ended up that we had been curving around toward the east, and we hit the highway at a point well north of where I thought we would. We had more than 4 miles of road walking before we reached Dairy Springs. With each step along that paved road, the railroad spikes in my pack got heavier and heavier. What had possessed me to pick them up in the first place? Now it was too late to discard them.

By the time we fetched the campground, I thought Fosco was going to lie down and expire. He kept muttering expletive-laced interrogatives like, "What kind of blankety-blank trail is this, where there is no blankety-blank trail?" I had never heard Fosco use such language.

Ironically enough, Fosco was being pummeled by the ease of our route, by its almost complete lack of vertical topography. Fosco had been training hard for several months before coming to Arizona, but all of his training had taken place in the heart of the Alps, where level terrain is about as common as bad chocolate and nonfunctional cuckoo clocks. On level ground, your gait stays fairly constant, and thus, redundancy-based problems, like a sock seam rubbing on one part of the heel, can transpire.

Fosco was limping badly, and when he pulled off his boots, I could not believe my eyes. He had the worst heel blister I have ever seen. This was not a blister as much as it was an open wound—and it was the size of Nebraska. It reached basically from the back of his knee down to the bottom of his heel, with its epicenter being located in the middle of his Achilles' ten-

Wooden fence near Kehl Spring,
Coconino National Forest

◆ ◆ ◆

don. Now, it's not like I haven't had my fair share of serious blisters. As a matter of fact, I have had some near-debilitating cases over the years and over the miles. And I have, in my hiking career, seen people with blisters that almost made me ill. But I had to take my hat off to Fosco here. He was now the Blister King. When he asked for my first-aid suggestions, I replied, "Surgery, if not outright amputation." There was not enough moleskin on earth to cover this poor man's malady.

Unfortunately, his camp shoes provided no relief. His only option was to walk around camp barefoot, and it was too chilly for that. To add insult to discomfort, it was still drizzling. Fosco set his tent up under a sprawling oak in the hope that it would keep him dry.

Rather than continuing to piece a route together through the trailless woods in the morning, I suggested to Fosco that we walk along the paved road as far as Mormon Lake Village before hooking into a series of dirt roads that would see us all the way to Blue Ridge Ranger Station, a day's walk from the famed Mogollon Rim. Fosco meekly concurred, too miserable to even ponder the matter. He seemed to appreciate the fact that I was trying to come up with hiking alternatives designed to ease his pain. I told him not to worry, as the instructions I had received from the Forest Service regarding the route from Mormon Lake to Blue Ridge were basically: "We don't know where the trail is going to go through that area, so make your way to Blue Ridge as best you can."

We stopped at the small store at Mormon Lake for a light snack. Mormon Lake is Arizona's largest natural body of water; but, as we were hiking along the highway, we could not help but notice that it was completely dry. There wasn't even a mud puddle in the middle.

IT REMAINED CLOUDY, cold, wet, and blustery for the rest of the afternoon and all the next day. The mud situation was getting worse and worse, as was Fosco's blister. I was torn between playing Johnny Cheerleader ("You know, it's nice to have a little cool weather for a change after all that heat and sun I experienced before you got here, Fosco." Or, "C'mon, Fosco, you can make it!") or keeping my mouth shut, letting my old friend suffer in silent dignity. By the end of Fosco's fourth trail day, he was ready to throw in the towel.

"I think I'll leave tomorrow and just go back to Switzerland," he said.

I said nothing in reply. There was nothing to say. I could not guarantee better weather; I could not guarantee that his foot would not get infected and fall off. I just tried to focus on positive thoughts, which was not hard for me, as I was not having a bad time at all. As far as I am concerned, if I am living free and easy with a pack on my back out in the woods, I am generally a pretty happy hombre. But my feet were feeling just fine, and I was out on the trail for sixty days, time enough to not be bothered by a few days of poor weather.

Soon after setting up my tent, I heated some water and walked off to wash up and change into less funky clothes. As I was scrubbing, I noticed a line of blue sky coming our way. I yelled at Fosco to look up. His visage transmogrified. He went from being the very definition of unhappy to sporting an ear-to-ear smile. The weather system that had followed us from Flagstaff was going along its merry way. Concomitant with the passage of the clouds was a severe drop in temperature, however. It got down to 15°F that night, but we both had enough gear to handle a little chilly weather.

The next day we had 18 miles of dirt road ahead of us. And, even though those roads were rougher by a factor of ten than most trails I have hiked, they at least passed through some of the most pleasant woods I have ever seen. I am certainly no forester, but I have spent enough time in various kinds of backcountry to recognize healthy stands of trees. The trees had breathing room between them, rather than being bunched up, and the species were mixed. There were trees of different sizes and ages living right next door to each other. A thoroughly integrated neighborhood.

Since we were hiking between 6,000 and 7,000 feet, the forest was dominated by pine and aspen. Fosco had read, before arriving in Arizona, that this was the largest continuous pine forest in the world. It certainly seemed to be so.

Many westerners live and breathe for the long view of life. We often look at trees as things that block our view of mountains or canyons. We do not see the trees or the forest as a spectacle in its own right. I began focusing on individual trees as I passed them, trying to take in the texture and individuality of their beauty the same way I did the Grand Canyon and the San Francisco Peaks. Of course, I might as well have done so, as there was little else to look at, save my feet or Fosco.

IT WAS ALMOST four o'clock—two hours before dark—when we arrived at Blue Ridge Ranger Station. Since it was Sunday, there was no one about. We filled our water containers from a nearby spigot and walked a few hundred yards away to camp. Again, it got down to 15°F. My water bag froze so solidly that it took two full days to get it thawed out—meaning I had to carry several pounds of ice with me on the trail.

Within minutes of leaving camp the next morning, we hooked into genuine trail. Our dirt road odyssey was behind us. We whooped and hollered and took photos of each other leaning against the first AZT sign we had seen in days. Soon thereafter we passed a hunter who told us to cinch down our packs because, shortly after passing Rock Crossing Campground, we had a 1,000-foot descent into Clear Creek Canyon, followed instantly by a 1,000-foot climb right back out of that canyon. As we were walking away, he asked, "Does the Arizona Trail go through the Mazatzal Mountains?"

"Why, yes, about two days south of Pine," I replied. "Why?"

Upper East Verde River, Tonto National Forest

This guy started making signs of the cross and asking the Lord to have mercy on our poor souls. He told us that the Mazatzals were the most fearsome and rugged mountains in the state and that we would rue the day we ever decided to step foot into that lofty range. He ran off without saying good-bye. It was almost like we had just told this man we were on our way to join a satanic cult.

Fosco and I looked at each other, perplexed, and moved on, actually eager to make our rendezvous with Clear Creek Canyon. The easy hiking we had been experiencing since Flagstaff was starting to bore us. Fosco and I both live in places where significant vertical topography dominates our physical and mental landscapes. We were looking forward to some ups and downs.

We began the circuitous descent into Clear Creek Canyon. As the canyon tightened, the area became more lush feeling and the tree species grew more varied and more dense. It was refreshing. Thing is, we got to the bottom in about five minutes. The man we passed earlier had only been about 900 feet off on his canyon depth estimate. It took another five minutes to hike out. This was sort of a letdown, but we did not let this letdown get us down. We were spurred on by the thought that, within a few hours, we would be standing atop the Mogollon Rim, a great geologic fault that stretches 200 miles southeast to northwest across the center of the state. Although 2,000 feet high in some places, the elevation would be 1,000 feet where we came upon it. The trail through here was well but inconsistently marked. For the most part, it was very easy to follow; but, several times we lost it in one timber cut or another, or while crossing one dirt road or another.

We started down into General Springs Canyon, which was a lovely surprise. There was a trickle of a glistening brook babbling through small Irish-green meadows. This was a place of utter tranquillity. I would not have been a bit surprised to round a bend and see a hobbit kicking back with a pipe in his mouth. Although we were sashaying so casually we were barely able to maintain our forward momentum, we soon left this memorable,

East Verde River, Tonto National Forest

◆◆◆

though short, section of trail at General Springs Historic Site, where we planned to camp. Boasting a restored cabin that once served as a stop-off point for people traveling along the Rim, the site consisted mainly of verdant meadows spreading for 100 yards in every direction. And those meadows were surrounded by knobby, pine-covered hills.

The one thing General Springs did not have was a very good spring. The creek we had been following through the canyon had trickled out about a half mile back. The only water we saw near the cabin was an inch-deep seep that was home to an impressive invertebrate population. Fosco and I went off in different directions, hoping to find something a little more potable.

My lucky find was a tent site that looked like it would hold the afternoon sun until the very last moment. Our gear was still wet from the heavy frost we experienced at Blue Ridge Ranger Station and it could use a quick airing. Fosco had better luck. He returned with two 1-gallon plastic jugs filled with water. Since neither of us had brought plastic water jugs with us, I assumed there must be some tale.

> **"There was a trickle of a glistening brook babbling through small Irish-green meadows. This was a place of utter tranquillity."**

"There is a small store right on the Rim," he said, smiling. "And," he said, "they sell beer." I thought I heard snippets of the *Hallelujah Chorus* being sung by the Vienna Boys Choir somewhere off in the distance.

"Well," I said, in an offhand way, "maybe I'll just mosey on over there and see what kind they've got." All thoughts of taking the time to dry my gear evaporated instantly.

Fosco then told me that he was a lying dog. That's not exactly how he worded it, but that's how his words were translated between my ears.

"I got the water from a couple of guys who were taking pictures of the Rim," he said, obviously not fathoming the depth and breadth of his treachery and soulless deception.

"Did they have beer?" I queried, almost in passing.

"I didn't ask them," my little Swiss enemy said.

"Well, let's go ask them now."

"They already left."

Just as I was about to poleax my companion, I realized that, as cold as it had been getting, a frosty beer was really the last thing I wanted at that moment. Fosco, therefore, yet lives.

So, we had 2 gallons of pure water, and life was good. Our gear dried quickly, and camp was sunny and comfortable. As soon as the sun went behind the trees, however, it cooled off so fast we could watch the mercury plummet on my little thermometer.

When we arose at 6 AM, it was 12°F. It's hard to move quickly when your fingers are numb and your glasses are fogged up. We didn't start hiking until well past seven.

The view from the Rim in the dawn light was awesome. The entire center part of the state opened up before us. Dale Shewalter had called this section the "mountainous heart of Arizona." He was not kidding. Off to the southwest lay the Mazatzals. And, yes, they looked intense.

And thus began one of the most poignantly yin-yang hiking days I have ever experienced. Every trail day has its trade-offs, its good and bad, its hard and easy aspects. To check out certain great views, you have to schlep a heavy pack into the mountains. Simple equation. This day, we had to tackle 19 miles along one of the hardest sections of the entire AZT, but the aesthetic rewards were off the scale.

Almost immediately after we dropped off the Rim, the trail began following the most serious stream I had seen since the Colorado River. It was the headwaters of the East Fork of the Verde River, which we would meet again in a few days. With each step down, another degree of chill left the air. By the time we reached Washington Spring it was almost hot. There was a great campsite right near the Verde. It is an understatement to say I was not

Crimson wildflowers, Tonto Natural Bridge State Park
◆.◆.◆

Pine Creek Falls,
Tonto Natural Bridge State Park
◆◆◆

Evidence of the extreme desert terrain that makes
up parts of the AZT
◆◆◆

happy with myself. Although General Spring was a nice place, we should have hiked down here the previous night. It would have been warmer and it would have put us 2 miles closer to Pine.

After a quick change from long pants to shorts, we hit the trail at a near gallop. I had told Fosco that, because the AZT between Washington Spring and Pine Trailhead followed the Highline National Recreation Trail, we would likely have smooth sailing for the entire day. I was incorrect.

Because the Highline Trail is more than 100 years old and because it was originally designed to carry horse and wagon traffic, it has suffered some severe erosion. It is one of the rockiest stretches of trail it has ever been my displeasure to stumble down for seven hours. At the same time, it goes down into and out of twenty-nine different small drainages. It was like hiking on a roller coaster track. I would much rather deal with one 5,000-foot ascent, followed by a 5,000-foot descent, than go up and down, up and down all the livelong day.

That was the yang. The yin side of the equation began with great views in every direction. The magnificent, cliff-faced Mogollon Rim was rarely out of sight, and numerous mountain ranges, including the Mazatzals, filled the entire southern horizon. At the bottom of many of the drainages into which we hiked were lovely little creeks. We were able to drink as much water as we wanted, as well as being able to run wet bandannas across our sweat-drenched brows every half hour or so.

The trail meandered into and out of every type of life zone this part of Arizona offers. It was like taking a tour of the state in miniature. At some points, we would be hiking through cactus-adorned slickrock. Five minutes later, we would be in the middle of a maple-dominated landscape that looked for all the world like New England in the fall. Then there would be sycamore-lined creek beds, followed by tall pine, followed by juniper and piñon. There were pools of cool water surrounded by moss-covered boulders, and huge stands of oak and open grassland. Even though we were both invigorated by the landscape, by mid afternoon we were running out of steam. When we got to a point where we could make out the highway to Pine off in the distance, we assumed we only had a mile or two left. Then we passed a trail sign that laid some startling bad news on us: It was still 4 miles to the trailhead. We were deflated. Before this point, I would have argued that it was impossible for any 15 miles of trail in the entire country to kick my posterior this thoroughly, but there it was: I could scarcely muster the energy to take another step. But muster that energy I did.

We both just gritted our teeth and pushed on. A hour later, we passed a sign telling us it was only 1 mile down to the trailhead. A longer mile has never existed. It was like we were in the middle of a massive non-Euclidean geometry experiment.

That last mile of trail was perfectly manicured and buffed. There was scarcely a loose pebble to be seen. Just when we saw the trailhead sign, we passed a family beginning a late-afternoon dayhike.

"*The trail meandered into and out of every type of life zone this part of Arizona offers. It was like taking a tour of the state in miniature.***"**

"Nice trail, huh?" the father asked, by way of an innocuous greeting. Fosco and I grunted by way of a halfhearted agreement.

By the time I took off my pack, I felt like a blacksmith had spent the better part of the day beating my ankles with a hammer. While Fosco waited at the trailhead, I walked a mile into town, where Fosco's rental car was parked. When I passed the Pine town limits sign, I made a mental note that I had just hiked my second 20-mile day along the AZT. That thought made me feel energized.

Then I realized that I only had 470 miles left on this hike. It was going way too fast.

Pine *to* Roosevelt Lake

◆.◆.◆.◆.◆.◆.◆.◆.◆.◆.◆

IT WAS ALREADY HOT AT 7 AM when we hoisted our packs next to the East Fork of the Verde River, two days south of Pine Trailhead. We should have started hiking two hours earlier. The main reason we did not was that I was kept awake most of the night by the endless howling, yapping, growling, yipping, and barking of the 300 dogs that live at the L.F. Ranch, next to whose property we camped.

It came as a disappointment to find this ranch here, although it was lovely and the owner was extremely friendly and helpful, and she kept her temper in check when we accidentally walked into her front yard. Many are the ranchers who would have voiced their justifiable displeasure at our trespass, no matter that it was unintentional. This lady just smiled, bade us welcome, and offered us use of her water spigot.

I had figured this would be the first night on my AZT hike that would find me camped next to flowing water in a legally designated wilderness area. I did not realize that there was an in-holder property right next to the Verde, right where the AZT crosses the river.

Fosco was obviously getting impatient with my languidness. He was ready to leave, as usual, almost immediately on gaining consciousness that morning. But, when I suffer from a poor night's sleep, which I often do, I cannot make myself move quickly. Actually, this is the second consecutive night that I have slept little. Back at Hardscrabble Mesa, where we camped

the previous night, several cows tromped around and through our camp from dusk until dawn, and a herd of hyperactive coyotes was throwing a fiesta nearby.

And this was it: the day we entered the infamous Mazatzals. Since our meeting with that hunter back near Blue Ridge Ranger Station, we have talked with two other people who spoke with a disconcerting combination of dread and awe about these mountains, the tallest of which is 7,904-foot Mazatzal Peak.

For several days we had been trying without success to get a handle on the water situation in the Mazatzals, most of which lie in one of the largest wilderness areas in the state—meaning we were unable to drop off a water cache any closer than Mount Peeley Trailhead, which was 35 miles away. We were told that Brush Spring, 5 miles from the Verde, might have water, but then again, it might not. Ditto Hopi Spring, 17 miles away. We could not begin our 3,000-foot ascent into the Mazatzals depending on "maybes," so we each carried 2 gallons of water.

From the ranch, the trail climbed steeply up an abandoned mining road. Fosco was in the lead, setting a steady pace. Without a doubt, he carries a heavy pack better than I do. I've always considered myself a fairly strong backpacker, but only when I am carrying less than about 45 pounds. I start losing efficiency, to say nothing of getting ornery, when I tote more than 45 pounds, and I figure my pack weighed about 50 pounds—16 of which was water—going into the Mazatzals.

◆◆◆

Sunset, Four Peaks Wilderness

Agave on high cliff, near Mount Peeley

❖❖❖

The sun was at head height as we ascended, and its intense light flashed through the adjacent trees like a strobe light. It was seriously disorienting. I had to stop several times to regain my senses, and I could tell by the look on my companion's face that he was thinking: *If we had left earlier, this wouldn't be so uncomfortable.* My shirt was completely soaked within thirty minutes, and within an hour I had sucked down 2 liters of water. This was clearly going to be a long day.

Our plan or, better stated, our hope was to make it 17 miles to Hopi Spring. If we either did not make it there, or if we did and it was dry, we would barely have enough water to make it to Mount Peeley Trailhead the next day. All told, this was a five-day, 93-mile stretch from Pine to Roosevelt Lake, where Fosco's hike with me will end.

About 2 miles from the river, we came across an ancient, mostly faded trail sign that pointed off into a dense, impenetrable-looking oak thicket 90 degrees from the road we were following. We wondered aloud about this sign's vintage and made mention of the fact that the trail to which it once belonged was obviously long gone. Then we read the sign: BRUSH SPRING. This sign marked our exit. This simply could not be. Fosco was nonplussed that I was even considering entering that thicket. I pulled out my topo maps and studied them. Fosco argued passionately that we ought to continue along the road we had been following since the Verde, just to make certain that there was not a new section of AZT up ahead.

After studying the maps, I made a decision to follow the old sign, and I had to play trip leader with Fosco. Back in Flagstaff we had talked about how every expedition, no matter how modest, has to have one leader and one leader only, and I told Fosco then and there that, in this instance, that person was going to be me. I told him that if I ever go hiking with him in the Alps, I would expect him to serve as leader. And I stressed that just because I was the leader of this little foray didn't mean I was going to be dictatorial. Fosco agreed with me on all counts, and on many occasions since he had joined me, we had based decisions on his observations and suggestions. But here, despite his passionate protestations, I simply felt that we needed to leave the road at this point.

It was a painful decision, as the "trail," which was in actuality a roadbed that must have been last used when mastodons roamed the continent, was completely infested with sapling-size foliage. It was like we were machete-ing our way through the dense jungle in some old black-and-white movie about Africa. Except that we didn't have machetes, and these trees all had skin-ripping stickers and/or pointed leaves. We had to bull our way through, bending back trees and pushing them out of the way while twisting our packs between the trunks and branches. This was combined with an uphill so steep that we found ourselves having to walk on our tippy-toes much of the time.

We did this for two long, painful hours. We were gradually moving toward a small saddle in a ridgetop. Fosco still had not bought into the idea that what we were doing was even remotely correct. He took advantage of every opportunity to call me an imbecile.

As we approached the ridge, we both thought the same thought: that there might be a nice, clear section of AZT up there and that it very well might have split off further up the original road we were walking on earlier. I hoped against hope that such would not be the case. From that moment on, I started mentally composing my apology speech to Fosco. But I still felt certain that my decision had at least not been wrong. There very well might be good trail up ahead, but I had figured out a way to get us where we were supposed to be, despite the fact that it had made for one of the least pleasant hiking experiences in a backpacking career that has spanned some 7,000 miles spread out over more than twenty years.

I almost danced the watuzi when we reached the saddle and found no signs of another trail. Fosco was understandably contrite.

"I guess I owe you dinner for doubting you," he said flatly.

"Well, Fosco, I could just as easily been wrong," I replied with false magnanimity. "I've been wrong before and I'll be wrong again. You just make sure you keep me in line."

I was really enjoying this.

But our ordeal was far from over. The dense foliage growing in the middle of the trail did not let up for at least another mile. One instant we were getting ripped to shreds by several captivating species of thorn-bearing plants, and the next we were standing in the middle of a completely de-nuded trail. This must have been the point at which the Forest Service trail crew had stopped hacking down saplings and undergrowth last season. It

was like escaping from a lion's cage. Our clothes were hanging in tattered strips, and our legs and arms looked like we had just auditioned for the part of Entree in a Ginzo knife commercial.

"WHAT ARE YOU DOING HERE, old friend?" I asked Fosco, out of the blue.

He hesitated. "After hearing you talk all these years about the long hikes you have taken, I wanted to give it a try," he said. "And I really like Arizona. What about you?"

"I do this for a living, and I'm lucky enough to make a living doing something that, overall, I like. I don't necessarily like every single moment; but, in the aggregate, I enjoy taking long hikes."

We both left it at that, knowing there's a lot more that could be said on the subject.

A mile later we arrived at Brush Spring, which had a great flow. It was more like a little river than a spring. This meant, of course, that we did not need to carry 2 gallons of water up from the Verde after all. We washed the wounds that covered every millimeter of our legs, topped off our water bottles, and reluctantly moved on.

Within a few hundred yards we encountered another section of trail covered with nearly impenetrable foliage. Although it did not last long, it was still discouraging, as I was a hurting unit. For the first time since I left Utah, the heat was killing me and my pack was so heavy it seemed like a full-grown cow had slipped into it before I left that morning. I spent the entire morning and early afternoon fixating on Fosco's back trying to keep up with him. He was dusting me.

Some days, you make good time, even when it feels like you're not; other days, you make bad time, even when it feels like that's exactly what you're doing. Sometime seemingly in the last century, we passed a sign that said: MAZATZAL DIVIDE TRAIL 3. I wondered if they measure distances in these parts by leagues or maybe by parsecs. We finally decided that we must have missed the Mazatzal Divide Trail junction. Twelve years later, we came across that junction. We were moving at slightly more than 1 mile per hour. Even factoring in the heat, the heavy packs, and the steep uphill, this was still a borderline embarrassing pace.

Sycamore in fall color along
Sycamore Creek, near Sunflower
❖ ❖ ❖

At one o'clock we came across yet another water source, which was not on the map. It was a rivulet in a rock-lined wash surrounded by tall pines. It would have made for an idyllic campsite, and we entertained briefly the idea of staying here, but that would give us something on the order of a 27-mile day to Mount Peeley Trailhead tomorrow, and that was out of the question.

By this point, the trail was wonderful to behold—the complete antithesis of the tree-covered route we followed earlier. Since once again we had topped off our water bottles, our packs were back up to 50 pounds and we were moving like we had just ingested a handful of Quaaludes.

> "*Some days, you make good time, even when it feels like you're not; other days, you make bad time, even when it feels like that's exactly what you're doing.*"

We wanted badly to make it to Hopi Spring, now figuring it would likely have water in it. But, after two more long ascents, we were spent. More accurately, I was spent. Fosco seemed to be doing fine. When we came across a flat spot on top of a small ridge at 3:30 that afternoon, we opted to stop for the day—some 3 miles short of Hopi Spring.

Once again, I had difficulty sleeping. This time, I found myself camped in the middle of a cricket convention. No sooner had I turned off my flashlight than the most raucous "cricketeering" I have ever heard commenced. I was tempted at one point to jump up and douse the entire area with stove fuel, with the idea of burning the buggers out; but, with my luck, this was the one place on earth where this particular species of cricket (probably, by the way, the endangered neurotoxic man-eating attack cricket) exists. In addition to starting a forest fire that surely would inflame the entire central part of Arizona, I would be prosecuted for eliminating the last vestiges of a once noble cricket species. *That* would surely work wonders for my outdoor-writing career. To make matters worse, sometime during the night I noticed that my inflatable sleeping pad was no longer inflated. It must have been punctured by some manner of thorn-bearing plant.

Sotol along the trail near Sunflower
❖ ❖ ❖

Wash running with snowmelt, Mazatzal Mountains
◆◆◆

I was packed and ready to go before Fosco was even up the next morning. I was not going to give the heat another opportunity to fry my spirit. We had 21 miles to go, and we began our day's hike with resolve and a no-nonsense gleam in our eyes.

We made it to Hopi Spring in less than an hour. It was flowing beautifully. If we had known about the water situation, we could have left the Verde with our usual complement of 3 liters. With 10 pounds less water on our backs, we could easily have made it to Hopi Spring the day before.

Although still overgrown in many areas, the Mazatzal Divide Trail was, overall, in splendid condition. Because we were carrying only 1 gallon of water each, we made very good time. As a matter of fact, we were almost sprinting. We knew we had four 1,000-foot-plus up-and-downs before reaching Mount Peeley Trailhead, and we were bound and determined to complete two of those ascent/descent combinations before noon.

We were now in the heart of the Mazatzal Wilderness. We were surrounded by some of the most forbidding-looking terrain we had seen so far, yet the trail itself did not reflect that terrain. It was well graded to the point of almost being benign. And we had lucked out, insofar as we were hiking in the shade all morning.

We passed within a mile of the Mazatzal Peak summit, which was gorgeous. This peak had personality. Its conical shape and colorful rock striations begged us to drop our packs and ascend it. It would have taken maybe an hour each way, but that would have to wait for another day. We did not have time to get to know this wonderful mountain better. Soon after passing Mazatzal Peak, we dropped our packs and ate lunch. It was noon and we had made our goal of knocking off two of the day's climbs. According to my GPS, we were only 4 miles from our supply cache at Mount Peeley Trailhead. We made it there four and a half hours later.

GPS coordinates can be deceiving. When I took my reading, I knew from my map that we were much farther than 4 hiking miles from Mount Peeley. The trail took an obvious large jog to the west. Still, it's a hard thing to deal with psychologically when you have seen that number four flash up on your GPS screen and, four-plus hours later, you still have not made it to camp.

The trail from Mazatzal Peak to Mount Peeley Trailhead was a marvel of engineering. In the middle of a mountain range that sports serious vertical

Blazing sunset seen from the Mazatzal Range, Four Peaks Wilderness

◆ ◆ ◆

Saguaro shrouded in fog, Tonto National Forest

◆◆◆

topography, the trail managed to stay on grade almost the entire way. Those who constructed it had figured out a way to get this path through the mountains for more than 10 miles without gaining or losing an inch. Of course, there was a price to pay: The trail meandered like few trails I have ever seen. If it had to travel to a ridge 5 miles away to keep from having to drop off into the valley below, it did so. And it did so dozens and dozens of times.

> "*We were now in the heart of the Mazatzal Wilderness. We were surrounded by some of the most forbidding-looking terrain we had seen so far, yet the trail itself did not reflect that terrain.*"

At 3 PM, I took another GPS reading. Two more miles. Even though our legs felt leaden, we were still moving fast. The trail was still in great condition, and through some sort of earth orientational miracle, we were still hiking in the shade. And it still took us 90 minutes to reach Mount Peeley Trailhead. Our outdated topo maps had lied to us. We never did have those last two 1,000-foot ascents and descents. This was good, as Fosco this day was as exhausted as I was the day before. He collapsed into a heap when we finally reached the pine-ringed campsite at Mount Peeley Trailhead, which is located at an elevation of slightly less than 7,000 feet. This marked my third 20-plus-mile day on the AZT, and I was feeling pretty chipper, or at least pretending to feel that way. I did not know then that we still had two more 20-milers ahead of us before reaching Roosevelt Lake.

I set up my tent on a small rise. Within ten seconds of bedding down, I learned that I had neighbors. A small, grassy knoll about 5 inches from where I laid my head was apparently home to the largest rodent population in Arizona. All night, I heard little creatures scurrying back and forth and squeaking. I'm certain they were saying, "Human alert!" all night long. This, combined with my airless Thermarest situation, produced yet another sleepless night. I got out of the tent at dawn feeling punch-drunk. Fosco got out of his tent with dread etched upon his face. He was beginning to wonder if he had it in him to make it to Roosevelt Lake. Although two weeks ago he started out pooh-poohing the difficulty of the AZT, I could tell he had developed a newfound, profound degree of respect for this trail and for the territory through which it passes.

According to the information I gleaned from the Forest Service, we were facing a 17-mile day. The first seven or so of those miles should be mostly downhill, as we descend from the Mazatzals to the Bushnell Tanks area, which is at less than 3,000 feet.

The trail was overgrown right out of the chute. By now, we had developed the ability to make comparative advantage decisions regarding the vegetation that grew alongside and over the trail. Certain species, like catclaw, were to be avoided at all costs; whereas others, like scrub oak, while unpleasant, were at least tolerable. We shucked and jived our way down the trail, turning and squirming to avoid making contact with some plants in favor of others. We were getting good at this.

The trail passed by several old mines, and Fosco, who would rather spend time in a cave than atop a mountain on a sunny day, dropped his pack and started exploring. Me, I am not partial to caves or mines. I really don't even like basements. Don't know whether it's claustrophobia or a preternatural fear of things underground. Either way, I waited in the shade of a sycamore grove while Fosco went into the mines. He returned exuberant. He saw bats and a few old mining implements. But, more than that, he had communed with the type and degree of darkness that can only be found beneath the surface of the earth.

I shook my head and hoisted my pack.

We expected to hit Highway 87 at Sycamore Canyon and walk down the highway 3 or 4 miles to Bushnell Tanks. We did not relish this thought, as Highway 87 (a major paved link from northern Arizona to metro Phoenix) is extremely busy. Just as we made out the highway against the backdrop of parched mountains to the east, we saw a trail sign. Ended up there was a brand-new section of trail, which eliminated the road walking completely. It added 3 or 4 miles to our day's hike, but it was much better than walking along a paved highway shoulder with endless cars whizzing by.

When we finally crossed the highway at Sunflower, it was 92°F, and I was wilted and fading fast. Once again, Fosco was hiking stronger than I was. I had to take a break less than a mile from our water cache.

Owl clover, lupine, and fiddleneck; Tonto National Forest
◆◆◆

Wildflowers, Tonto National Forest

◆◆◆

Actually, I was impressed with how well Fosco was doing. His blister, which he had been fastidiously treating topically with a Swiss herbal concoction named something like "essence of mungwort root," was almost completely healed, and his strength and endurance were increasing with each passing day. Moreover, he seemed to be coming to positive terms with trail life. He seemed happy and fulfilled. I don't know if he was having fun, but I guessed that he was feeling rewarded for his efforts. I was pleased about that.

The Bushnell Tanks area, which follows Sycamore Creek, is one of the prettiest areas in Arizona. Completely lined with lofty sycamores—one of the most lovely tree species in the West—it is shaded and tranquil. It is also completely ruined. If there is ever a thing by which I will judge the Tonto National Forest Powers That Be, it will be that they have allowed the area bordering Sycamore Creek to be so ravaged. This is dirt biker and four-wheeler territory, and never have I seen public property so negatively impacted by recreationists. The number of trash-filled, denuded campsites was staggering, and each campsite had at least one fire ring. For 2 solid miles—until this lovely little creek fades away—there is nothing but hideous evidence of unconscionable destruction of the natural world. ATVs, ORVs, and dirt bikes have torn apart huge swatches of vegetation on every surrounding hill. Signs are shot to pieces. Mesquite trees have been cut down for firewood.

Fosco was stunned. Like most Europeans, he does not know whether to consider the United States a first-world or a third-world country. Here, there was little doubt in his mind.

"Sometimes, I don't even consider you people civilized," he said, as he bitterly surveyed the abysmal scene at Bushnell Tanks.

I had placed our water cache beyond the thickest concentration of campsites. That meant we were past the creek and the sycamores. We searched for a decent spot near the cache, but everywhere we looked there were piles of cans, broken bottles, discarded clothing, and even furniture.

We ended up pitching our tents right next to the shadeless dirt road, and for most of the evening four-wheelers driven by men carrying sidearms passed to and fro at high speed. The dust never settled.

As dusk descended, someone farther up the road started firing a rifle and he or she continued doing so for more than an hour. It was like we were camped in the middle of the *Road Warrior*, except that *Road Warrior* was a lot more laid back and quiet.

We starting hiking well before dawn on Fosco's last trail day. We had been forewarned by a dayhiker we passed on the other side of Highway 87 that there were no trail signs in the Bushnell Tanks area and that the AZT was consequently very difficult to locate. Ordinarily, when armed with that kind of information, I would have scouted the situation out before retiring the night before. But I was too tired to do so, and Fosco and I soon paid the price for my slothfulness. As trip leader, it is my job to locate the trail, and I let us down. We spent a full-paced ninety minutes searching for any sign of the AZT, only to end up within 100 yards of our campsite. Thus, we had 4 or 5 miles under our belt before even beginning the 17-mile trek to Lone Pine Saddle, where Fosco's rental car was parked. By the time we finally figured our situation out, the air temperature was more than 90°F.

" *The trail from Mazatzal Peak to Mount Peeley Trailhead was a marvel of engineering. In the middle of a mountain range that sports some serious vertical topography, the trail managed to stay on grade almost the entire way.* "

The trail climbed for 7 miles straight up alongside Boulder Creek, which was completely water free. We busted through head-high plant life every step of the way. It was rough going. When we finally made it to Forest Road 22, there was a sign letting the world know that the route we just followed was for mountain bikers as well as hikers. I would pay money to see a mountain biker descend the trail we just came up.

We followed Forest Road 22, which hugged the ridgetop of the last vestige of the Mazatzals, for 12 miles. The hike was arduous in that the road consisted of little more than one steep uphill/downhill combination after another.

But there was that yin-yang thing at work and play again. In spite of the tortuous trail, we hiked near some splendid rock formations, and the views of the approaching Four Peaks Wilderness were awesome. As we got

The trail, snaking its way from Four Peaks Wilderness
◆·◆·◆

Cirrus clouds drift over the trail, Tonto National Forest
◆◆◆

closer to Four Peaks, we entered another massive burn area, and we stayed in that burn area, which spread as far as the eye could see in every direction, all the way to the car.

Even though we had only hiked 17 official trail miles, because of our route-finding *faux pas* that morning, we had put in yet another 20-plus-mile day. A Forest Service person had told us that, because of the damage done by the burn, the trail from Lone Pine Trailhead down to Roosevelt Lake, which now spread beneath us to the east, was impassable. So we loaded our packs into the car and began the drive down to the lake.

I glanced over at Fosco. He was sunburned, cut, and scratched, and he had bags under his eyes the size of pillows. But he was already talking about taking his next long backpacking trip.

"You know, I calculated that the distance we have traveled since Flagstaff is the equivalent of hiking the entire width of Switzerland," he said.

"I think maybe I'll start thinking about doing that hike. Want to go?"

"Sure, Fosco, you can count on me," I replied halfheartedly, while dozing off in the passenger seat.

There was melancholy in the air. Fosco would soon be on his way home. His trip along the AZT was over and done. He was already at the point where he was putting a positive memory spin on his experiences. He was mentally concocting the tales he would tell his family and friends back in Ticino.

It was sad to think that in a couple of days I would return to the AZT by myself. But that's how it works with me. No matter what, I will always return to the trail alone. I accept both the good and the bad implications of that reality.

As we drove, Fosco congratulated me on being at the halfway point in my hike. Only 370 miles to go. That thought did not make me happy.

Hackberry Creek Canyon, Mazatzal Range
◆◆◆

Roosevelt *to* Oracle

STANDING A FEW HUNDRED yards up the trail from Theodore Roosevelt Dam, I could see Fosco driving away in his Geo. As his car went out of sight, I felt a little hollow. Fosco had proved to be a more-than-adequate trail companion, and his company would be sorely missed. This was an out-of-character observation on my part, as just about every other time in my life that I have been left by myself on the trail, I have felt happy and free. Not this time.

The 6-mile stroll to Cottonwood Spring caught me completely by surprise. Since I was climbing into the Superstition Mountains, I figured that I was about to enter some of the roughest and least-forgiving desert in the state. *Au contraire.* The trail to Cottonwood was well shaded and lovely, and the spring had enough of a flow that it should have been called a creek. I lingered at the spring site and wished that I had planned to camp here, but I had placed three 1-gallon jugs of water a few miles ahead. That way, all I had to do was crush the jugs and carry them out with me—meaning I would not have to drive all the way around here from Superior to retrieve my usual water and food cache containers.

This was my shortest trail day so far, but it was good to take it easy. I had hiked 108 miles my last six trail days, and I was feeling beat up. My ankles hadn't yet recovered from the rocky section between General Springs and Pine. And I have an old knee problem—a strained medial collateral ligament gained from Tae Kwon Do—that was flaring up painfully. It was time to throttle back for a week, and that's exactly what I did.

I planned on taking four leisurely days to make the 41 miles from Roosevelt to Superior, before deciding what to do between there and Oracle. There's a 60-mile gap south of the Gila River where there is no AZT, and I had been vacillating the entire trip about whether to hike along dirt roads for that stretch to maintain my continuity or simply to blow off that section of the trek.

As I was kicking house-size cowpies out of the way so that I could set up my tent, I disturbed several scorpions. It was astounding to think that no one had forewarned me to keep my eyes peeled for these nasty little animals. But this is not the first time I have interacted with scorpions. Far from it. In my extensive desert travels—in this country and abroad—I have had plenty of dealings with these venomous arachnids. While sleeping *sans* tent down in Chihuahua one time, I woke up with one sitting on my chest, staring me right in the eye. And I almost got stung on the butt once while visiting an old outhouse in the Dominican Republic. I am determined to keep my eyes peeled here, as I have seen what scorpion stings can do to hands and feet.

Even though my campsite was not the best, it was still nice to kick back for an afternoon in camp. I pulled out my camp chair and took in the wonderful vistas that surrounded me in every direction. This was saguaro cactus territory, and few plant species are as noble or as beautiful. Once you get past the realization that seemingly the entire species is making an obscene gesture toward the entire world, saguaros come across as grandfatherly. It seems that, with a little prodding, they ought to be able to impart some wisdom on a schmuck like me. But if

A heavy stand of saguaro cactus with the snow-covered Sierra Ancha Mountains in the distance

Predawn light on Roosevelt Lake, Tonto Basin
◆.◆.◆

there isn't the saying "Never prod a saguaro" in the Southwest, then there should be.

I spent four straight hours just parked there, watching the afternoon light work its magic on the saguaros and the parched foothills of the Superstitions. I kept looking up the trail, feeling like someone was soon going to walk into my camp. Few times in my life has this feeling of impending company been stronger. Although I have been on the AZT now for more than 350 miles, with the exception of the Grand Canyon I have yet to pass another backpacker. I have passed a handful of mountain bikers, a few dayhikers, and hundreds of hunters, but that's it. No kindred spirits.

With Fosco's example still fresh in my mind, I was up and at 'em well before dawn, and on the trail before the sun cleared the eastern horizon. It was cool, but there was no doubt soon such would not be the case. The sky was cloud free. Within minutes of camp, a couple of hunters pulled up behind me in their pickup truck. They stopped and we chatted for a spell.

The entire time I was along the AZT, I was caught off guard by how friendly the hunters were.

"This is some beautiful country, ain't it?" one of the hunters asked, as he leaned on the hood of his Ford.

"Yes, it is," I agreed.

There was a moment when no one spoke, when the three of us just stood there taking in the early morning beauty of central Arizona. Then I said adios and moved on.

Halfway up the first hill, just before the Superstition Wilderness boundary, I finally crossed paths with a backpacker. He had stayed at a small stock tank less than a half mile from my campsite. It was eerie to think that the entire previous afternoon I had expected to run into another hiker.

Long-distance backpackers can recognize each other instantly. This man was in his late forties, and I could tell from his demeanor, his hiking technique, and the "rattiness" of his gear and his clothing that this was not

Evening light on the Sierra Ancha Mountains and Roosevelt Lake, Tonto National Monument

◆◆◆

View of Apache Lake at sunset from Two Bar Ridge
◆◆◆

Saguaro reflected in Happy Camp Creek, Tonto National Forest

◆·◆·◆

his first hiking trip. Far from it. During the kind of condensed conversation hikers have when they pass on the trail, he told me that he had hiked the entire 2,100-mile Appalachian Trail the summer before. In ninety days. My jaw dropped. Either this man was exaggerating, which would be a breach of hiker's etiquette so severe that I do not even care to ponder it, or this man was one stud hiker. It took me 147 days to hike the Appalachian Trail, and I was not exactly dogging it.

As we exchanged basic AZT skinny, he told me to prepare myself, as the trail was severely overgrown with catclaw through the Superstitions. I groaned. My leg wounds had not yet healed from the Mazatzals. I told him what he was up against, and we moved on.

The entire conversation took less than five minutes.

"*This was saguaro cactus territory, and few plant species are as noble or as beautiful.*"

Although the trail was overgrown somewhat, this was minor league compared with the Mazatzals. The trail was in good condition as it wound its way over arid ridgetops and down into dry washes—desert country at its most wonderful. I only planned to go 13 miles to Reavis Creek, which I was assured actually held water. A night next to a creek in the middle of a wilderness area. I couldn't wait.

Fosco's plane was scheduled to leave Phoenix's Sky Harbor at 10 AM. At 10:05 I looked up and saw a jet passing way overhead. The chances of that being Fosco's plane were remote. Nonetheless, I waved my arms, wondering if it was possible to make out a lone body standing down here in the endless Arizona backcountry. I doubted it, although with my luck someone in that plane would have seen me waving my arms and used an airplane phone to call the local search-and-rescue group, telling them they had seen a hiker signaling for help.

The hiking got a little harder as the drainages the AZT crossed got steeper and deeper. And it was, once again, hot as blazes. I started dashing between small patches of shade as the sun climbed higher and higher into the deep blue sky. At the same time, the trail was getting rockier and more eroded. Once more, I found myself hiking cautiously, tensely, and defensively. I could not purge the feeling that I was going to suffer an ankle injury while on the AZT. My pace became glacial as the trail became a veritable quarry of loose rock.

By the time I saw the trees lining Reavis Creek, I was beat. Any form of exercise is best done in a relaxed fashion, and I was not relaxed. Tense muscles get tired faster, and I was walking, talking evidence of that reality. Anyone passing me on the trail would have guessed that I had sometime in the recent past suffered a spinal injury and was told I would never walk again, and I was out on the trail for no other reason than to prove the doctors wrong, even though I could barely put one foot in front of the other. Harrison Ford's rehabilitation scenes in *Regarding Henry* sprung to mind.

Reavis Creek was paradise found—an oasis in the heart of one of Arizona's most formidable mountain ranges, which is saying a mouthful. Flowing through the middle of an old ranch site, Reavis Creek was lined with cottonwood and sycamore in the height of fall color. The trail passes through the middle of an orchard, and apples were everywhere. A sweet smell hovered in the air. This place was Eden-esque, and potential tent sites were in abundance.

I decide to hike as far as I can along the creek before the water fizzles out, as it always does in this state. I find a grassy spot at the edge of an orchard, behind a stand of leafless, spindly trees I cannot identify. I go down to the creek to wash up and to fill my water bag. The creek is small, but it contains several thigh-deep pools, and the water is cool enough to be refreshing. As I wash, I realize that one of my toenails has just come off. That's one of the prices long-distance hikers often pay: We lose a lot of toenails because of the constant banging of tootsies against boots. From the look of things, I will lose at least two more before this hike is over.

As I am preparing dinner, a pack-laden couple ambles by. I can tell from a distance that these people are not long-distance hikers. Their gear is

Much of the AZT, which is still under construction, follows old roads.

◆•◆

too clean and their grooming habits have not deteriorated completely. They have just come in for the night from some trailhead I've never heard of. While we hobnob, I notice that the man is sporting a walking cast on one leg. Ends up he broke his foot; but, since he and his wife were on vacation, he was not going to let a little excruciating pain deter him from visiting this wonderful place.

I was impressed.

As he walked away, I noticed that he had an extra hiking boot lashed to his external-frame pack. He was carrying the boot that ordinarily he would wear on his broken foot. Wonder why. Symmetry? Optimism?

It got down to a very refreshing 28°F that evening, and there was frost on the ground when I got up before dawn. While taking my morning stroll into the woods, I came upon a horrible sight. There was poison ivy everywhere. I almost ran shrieking out of the Superstitions. I am as allergic to poison ivy as a person can be and not die of anaphylactic shock after catching it. No, I'm not that fortunate. I continue to live when I catch poison ivy. I have had scalp-to-toes, back-to-front cases that have amused dermatologists from coast to coast, and if there is so much as a sprig of this cursed, wretched plant in the same time zone as yours truly, it will somehow manage to find its way into my underwear.

This turn-of-flora-events did not make me happy.

The hike out of Reavis Ranch, on the other hand, did. The trail followed the creek up to a small saddle, and the whole while, it passed through knee-high meadows with the softest grass I have ever touched. Covered with cooling dew, the grass tickled my legs for several miles. The trail was relatively rock free, well graded, and amply shaded. It was a joy to walk upon.

As I descended into Rogers Canyon, I started passing dozens of dayhikers, horsepackers, and, yes, even backpackers. I could not believe my eyes. I talked to a couple of the dayhikers and they told me that this is one of the most popular hiking destinations for metro Phoenix dwellers. These

Happy Camp Creek, Tonto National Forest
◆.◆◆

guys were going to some Indian ruins a few miles off the AZT. I didn't realize there were any Indian ruins in the vicinity. That's one of the problems
with taking a long hike. You get so focused on the trail that you don't pay
enough attention to things close to the trail.

The Rogers Trough Trailhead was packed. Four ladies were preparing
for a dayhike, and as I chowed down one of my wife's homemade trail bars,
which are veritable neutron stars of calories and nutrients, one of the women
ambled over. I asked her why I had not passed more hikers on the AZT.

She responds that, for most Arizonans, hiking season is only now
beginning. Early November is when packs and boots get pulled out of the
closet and dusted off. She said I should see some of the places through
which I had passed in mid winter.

> **"Reavis Creek was paradise found—an oasis in the heart of one of Arizona's most formidable mountain ranges, which is saying a mouthful."**

"There will be a lot of people in the Mazatzals in December, January,
and February," she said.

Made perfect sense to me.

I had 2 miles of dirt road walking between Rogers Trough and
Montana Mountain. The road was steep, rutted, and rocky, but the views
extended almost to Phoenix, which on the one hand was interesting enough,
but on the other hand was sickening. As pretty as the landscape was, the
pollution was horrendous. Sickly, brown air covered the world as far as I
could see.

I hiked on, and at Montana Mountain the trail picked up again and
began its 3,000-foot drop into Trail Canyon. The sun was oriented in such a
way that I could hear my lips frying like bacon. It was a scorcher, and the
descent was long. When it ended, the trail followed the bottom of a dry wash
for several miles. There are few kinds of hiking I enjoy more than following
small washes. The going can be slow because of all the loose sand, but
washes present a subtle form of beauty found in few other places. Here you

can see the fundamental forces of geology at work on a palpable scale. Sure, you can conceive of erosion in the Grand Canyon, but the scale there is overwhelming. Trail Canyon is a Grand Canyon in miniature, a Grand Canyon waiting to happen.

I had a water cache on the side of a dirt road 12 hiking miles from Reavis Creek. I had decided that if I arrived at the cache before 2 PM I would go ahead and hike 8 more miles into Superior, where my truck was parked at the police station. I was fatigued down to my bone marrow, and I needed a few days of rest and relaxation. Since I left Utah more than a month earlier, I had not had a real day off. Every day had been spent either hiking or dealing frantically with logistics.

> "*There are few kinds of hiking I enjoy more than following small washes. The going can be slow because of all the loose sand, but washes present a subtle form of beauty found in few other places.*"

When I arrived at my cache, there were four hunters there. Their site looked like a refugee camp in Zaire. Gear was strewn everywhere, and their beer can pile was so tall it should have been named, surveyed, and included on the next generation of maps of this area. These boys looked like they had been sucking down brewskis, well, basically since the day they were born. Their noses were crimson and swollen, their complexions ruddy, and their eyes redefined the concept of bloodshot. They also happened to be very friendly and cheery. Before I even finished greeting them, they were quick to, first, offer me a cold can of Bud and, second, to assure me that the mess I was eyeballing discreetly would be cleaned up before they left. What did I look like, the litter police?

The hunters said I could leave my pack with them while I walked those 8 long, hot miles into Superior. Without the pack, it took me only two hours to do so. When I returned, the men were out in the field, as they told me they would be. On top of my pack was a note:

A hiker pauses in White Canyon Wilderness

Evening light on the cliffs and peaks of White Canyon Wilderness

◆ ◆ ◆

Boulders near a future site of the AZT, Tortilla Mountains

◆◆◆

A hiker on the AZT near Oracle
◆·◆·◆

Dear hiker:
There's more beer in the cooler. Help yourself. You are more than welcome to
stay the night with us. Good luck on your journey. It was nice talking with
you. And we WILL clean up all the trash!

An hour later I was happily ensconced in a motel room in the nearby town of Globe, and I pretty much did not leave that room for two days. During that time I talked on the phone to several AZT people, and I decided to blow off that 60-mile trailless section between the Gila River and the town of Oracle. I had too many body parts paining me too badly to spend four days hiking along dirt roads that do not have, and never will have, anything to do with the AZT.

Instead, I dayhiked the section between Superior and the Tonto National Forest boundary near Ajax Mountain, then drove around and day-

hiked the section through the starkly lovely White Canyon Wilderness area—although I never was certain that I was on the AZT in this area.

As I drove past the Gila River toward Oracle, through the open-pit copper-mining capital of the known universe, a severe-looking weather front began to bear down on central Arizona. It got cold fast, and the rain came in droves.

Thus I came, in my truck instead of on my feet, to the town of Oracle, which is famous for two things: for being the sometimes home of the late Edward Abbey and for being home to the Biosphere II facility.

I now only had two sections of trail left.

It was time to start savoring every moment, every inch. For soon—far too soon—this journey would be a thing of my past.

View of the Galiuro Mountains across the San Pedro River valley, Coronado National Forest

❖·❖·❖

Oracle *to* Saguaro National Park

◆.◆.◆.◆.◆.◆.◆.◆.◆.◆.◆

SOMEWHERE BETWEEN Superior and Oracle lies the transition between central and southern Arizona. I could feel, almost taste, Old Mexico—*mia pais segunda*—getting closer. There was a waft of tamales, one of mankind's greatest creations, in the wind.

I was leaving what Dale Shewalter had called "the mountainous heart of the state," but that did not mean I was leaving the mountains. Far from it. The massive Santa Catalinas lay before me. This is the loftiest range I will have visited since the San Francisco Peaks north of Flagstaff. Mount Lemmon, the highest peak in the Catalinas, is more than 9,200 feet high.

These mountains also *feel* different from the Superstitions or the Mazatzals. And the feeling is laced with contradiction; for, even though I am moving farther south, the Catalinas, because of their height, seem more northern. There's even a ski area atop Mount Lemmon, and near the ski area there's an alpinelike village, Summerhaven, that is dominated by chateau-type architecture.

Now I am in Oracle—Ed Abbey's old stomping grounds, at least part of the time. Maybe. I must have asked fifteen people in Oracle where old Cactus Ed resided, and I witnessed several world records being set in the areas of evasion and subject changing. It seemed that people simply did not want to talk about Oracle's most famous citizen. Communities often protect their writers, as well they should.

North of Oracle, in plain view, lie the Catalinas—massive and foreboding. And to the east lies the massive and foreboding San Manual open-pit copper mine and smelter. From many places in town you can see the mine's chimney, 10 miles distant, belching smoke. An amazing dichotomy: one of the state's most beautiful mountain ranges filling one vista, and one of the nastier extractive industries on earth filling another.

Beginning this day, I am the houseguest of Frank and Laurie Hogg, and their eight-year-old daughter, Emily. Frank is the assistant director of the Oracle State Park's Center for Environmental Education, through which 6 miles of the AZT passes. Frank is passionate about the trail and spends a lot of free time working on it. As a matter of fact, the AZT crosses the property where he lives.

For two nights, I feel as though I am cheating. I have a soft couch on which to sleep and use of the Hoggs' shower, kitchen, TV, and bookshelf. All of which is good, because the weather has been aggressively abysmal. It has been deluging for several days now, and the wind has been gale force.

Frank has made arrangements for me to dayhike the first section of trail south of Oracle. He gives me a ride to the trailhead at Oracle State Park. From there, I stroll the 11 miles back up to his house, where I once again spend the night, before heading full bore into the Catalinas. It's about 80 miles from Oracle to the eastern edge of Saguaro National Park, where my truck awaits me, and I plan on taking six days to hike that distance.

Oracle State Park is not yet technically open to the public. It is an old ranch site that was bequeathed to the state for use as an environmental

◆◆◆

View across Sycamore and Bear Canyons, Santa Catalina Mountains

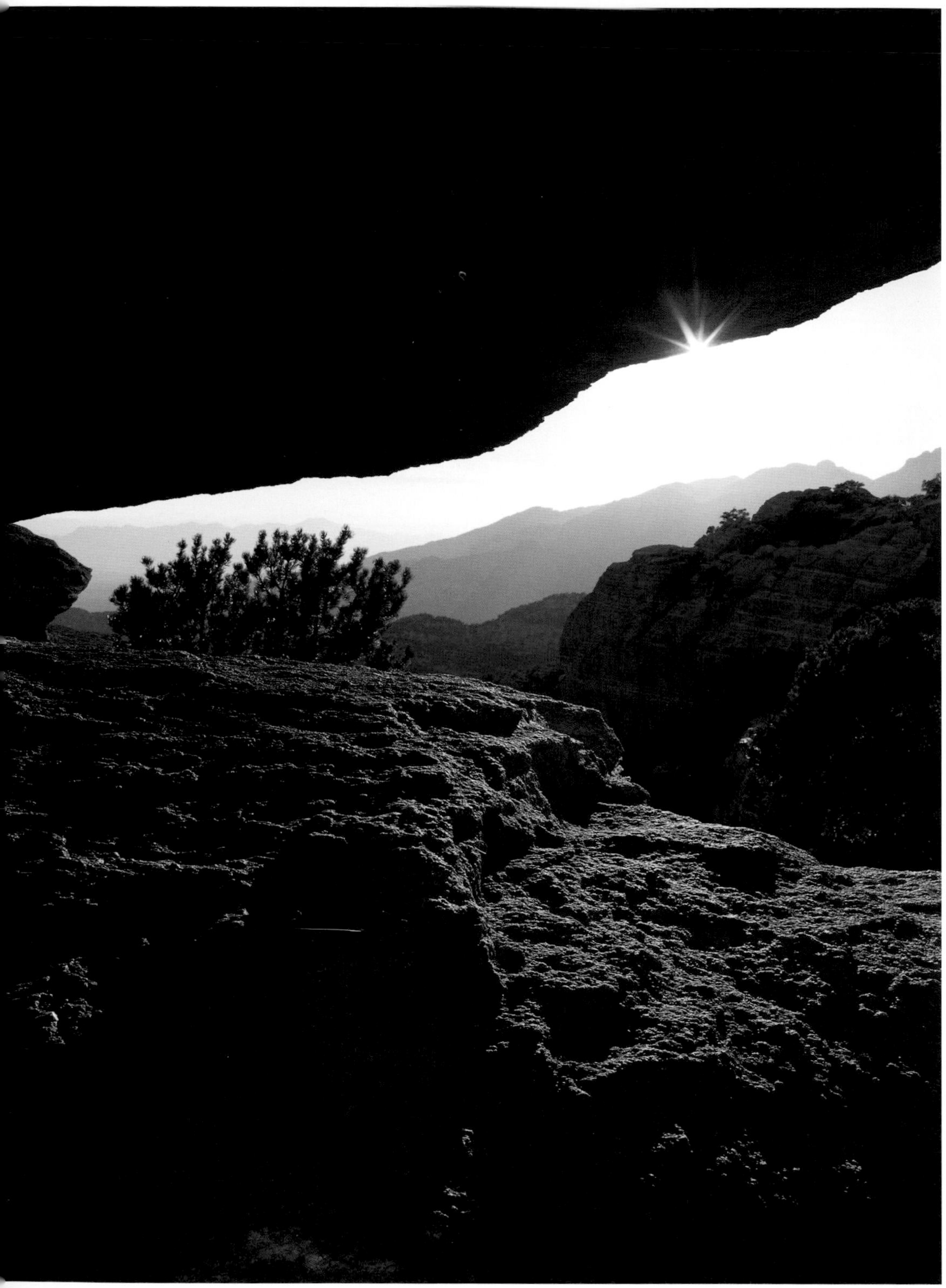

Sunset in the Pusch Ridge Wilderness, Santa Catalina Mountains

Melting snow cascades into Upper Bear Canyon, Coronado National Forest

interpretive and educational center, and for the past several years its small, hardworking, and dedicated staff has been toiling to set things up for the as-yet-unscheduled Grand Opening.

The AZT through the park will be used as an educational tool, and thus its design concept is somewhat different from other sections of the trail. It seems that every inch of the trail here has been meticulously planned. Although most other sections of trail are well conceived on the macro scale, this one has been well conceived on the micro scale. The difference between the AZT through Oracle State Park and, say, the section north of Grand Canyon National Park is the difference between a Robert Bly poem and a story about the Cardinals in the sports section of the *Arizona Republic*. Certainly, I would not want the AZT to be thusly designed all the way from Utah to Mexico, in the same way that I do not desire to read Robert Bly poetry all the time.

But it sure made for a pleasant diversion.

This section of the AZT set a new standard for meandering. It went out of its way to switchback through everything even remotely interesting in the state park. It traversed many different life zones, from sage-covered fields to juniper-piñon-dominated hillsides to exposed cactus-covered ridgetops to the sandy bottoms of washes. Since I was not encumbered with a pack, I was able to take my time and enjoy the fine, detailed work performed by Hogg and his associates. I was disappointed when the trail left the park and began the climb up Oracle Ridge, on the side of which the Hoggs dwell.

The weather was flat out foul, and it showed no signs of getting less foul. I had briefly entertained the thought of picking up my pack at Casa de Hogg and putting in a few more miles before nightfall, but I had no desire whatsoever to expose myself to these elements. That's the thing about Arizona: Most of the time—nay, the overwhelming majority of the time—the weather is astoundingly wonderful; but when it's nasty, it's real nasty. Sure, some of that is relative, in that anytime the weather here is not perfect, it's considered bad; but a lot of it is absolute as well. Like this day would be considered miserable anywhere on earth. Aleutian Island dwellers would batten down the hatches and stay inside if such weather visited their home territory.

That night, the weather deteriorates even more. The rain does not let up even slightly, and I lie awake most of the night dreading the dawn. Frank

and Laurie try to convince me to stay another day, but I've been relaxing too much this past week and feel like I'm losing my AZT momentum.

At 7 AM I hoist my pack and head out into the heart of the climatic funkiness. Although I hit the trail in shorts, I'm wearing my Gore-Tex jacket and it is cinched down. I have my hood string drawn so tight I can barely see the trail in front of me; peripheral vision is out of the question. This is drudge hiking at its finest—putting one foot in front of the other in the hope that, sometime soon, the weather will break.

The trail goes 4,000 vertical feet up the spine of Oracle Ridge in about 10 miles. The going is steep and, because of the rain, the footing is slick and treacherous. And I am moving so slowly I'm almost sliding backward, back down into Oracle. I feel dizzy, light-headed, disoriented, extremely tired, and achy. I am also concerned, for I do not have a firm water plan for this night, which seems ironic in the middle of a downpour.

> "*That's the thing about Arizona: Most of the time—nay, the overwhelming majority of the time—the weather is astoundingly wonderful; but when it's nasty, it's real nasty.*"

My intent is to hike to Dan Saddle, from where I will drop all the way down into Cañada del Oro, losing almost every foot of elevation I have gained on this slog up Oracle Ridge. All told, it should be about a 15-mile day, which isn't too bad, except that it is likely that there won't be any water in Cañada del Oro. I was told by a Forest Service employee several months earlier that there would be water down there, but Frank (as well as several other people) begged to differ. And from the bottom of Cañada del Oro, it's

Bigtooth maple leaves, Pusch Ridge Wilderness
◆◆◆

15 more miles up and over yet another ridge of the Catalinas to the next reliable water source. That makes a total of 30 water-free miles, unless, of course, you count the rain.

When there's a gap between one cloud bank and the next moving in from the west, I can make out the Biosphere II facility on the valley floor far below. Par for its conceptual course, it looks like something straight out of a science fiction flick. I would love to visit the place sometime, mainly because I cannot fathom what would make a person want to get locked up in a small building for two straight years.

The weather finally begins to break. At last I loosen my hood string and realize that I am hiking through a serious stretch of splendid rock formations that form the spine of Oracle Ridge. Cañada del Oro spreads out beneath me. *Way* beneath me. I pull my pack off and rest at Dan Saddle. I still feel terrible. Up until now, I have just assumed that I am tired and achy because, well, I am in the middle of a two-month hike and I'm beginning to wear down. At Dan Saddle it finally sinks in that I am officially ill. If I felt like this back home, I would assume that I was coming down with the flu. I would whimper and guilt my spouse into pampering me.

I check out the map and realize that the old AZT route goes 3 miles straight ahead to Summerhaven (where there are several motels), while the new route drops down into Cañada del Oro. The new route was established two years earlier to guide hikers around the Mount Lemmon area, which is heavily used and heavily impacted. As I was sitting there vacillating between following the official route and getting my sick carcass into a motel room, a couple of horsepackers rode up from Cañada del Oro. They told me they had seen nary a drop of water in the canyon. My decision was made. Three fairly easy miles later, I found myself checking into the Summerhaven Lodge. After a large lunch, I went back to my room and slept for the entire afternoon.

Heavy spring runoff swells a waterfall in Sabino Canyon
♦.♦.♦

I HAD A LONG NIGHT, alternating between shirt-soaking sweats and bone-deep chills. I got up several times to take a shower to cool off or heat up, depending on which temperature extreme was ravaging my *corpus delecti* at a given moment. I fully expected to take another day off to recover, but when dawn broke frosty and frigid over Summerhaven, I felt fine and dandy. I moseyed on over to the local cafe for a hearty breakfast consisting mainly, though not solely, of the best French toast I have ever eaten. And, since it was an all-you-can-eat affair, I consumed it in proverbial mass quantities. Then I waddled back to the lodge, picked up my pack, waddled down to Marshall Gulch Trailhead, and from there hiked on a wide and smooth trail into the wild Pusch Ridge Wilderness.

The sky was completely clear, and the surrounding pine forest was snow covered from where I stood all the way to the summit of Mount Lemmon. I could see my breath as I hiked. It was hard to believe I was in southern Arizona.

After a very pleasant walk down the aptly named Wilderness of Rocks Trail, I intersected the new AZT route a few miles up from Romero Pass. I was in the middle of some seriously rugged terrain, with rocky cliff faces dropping off in every direction. Below, the western and northern edges of metro Tucson spread out to the horizon. Man, I remember Tucson when it was little more than a town. Now, it is a bona fide metropolis, one of the fastest-growing cities in the nation.

You know you're in for a captivating descent anytime that your *approach* to the place where your descent commences is knee-wrackingly intense. The drop into Romero Pass took an hour, and from there I had to descend another 2,000 feet into the Sabino Canyon complex. During that descent, which was spread out over 5 miles, I went from snow to saguaros. It was like driving from Canada to Mexico in sixty minutes.

Since the canyon was so tight, there was plenty of shade, and therefore the vegetation was thick. Too thick, as a matter of fact. Catclaw covered much of the trail, and in many places there was poison ivy reaching out like its only goal in life was to grab my legs specifically. Although I worked hard to avoid making any contact with that most loathsome of plants, I knew my efforts were futile. There was simply no way to make it down the trail without touching some of those shimmering leaves.

There are many inaccuracies circulating about poison ivy. One is that all you have to do is be touched by one of the leaves to catch it. Actually, the leaves have to be compromised. The active ingredient in poison ivy is an acid called urushiol. It courses through the plant's circulatory system like blood. Unless an insect chews a wound in a leaf or a stem is broken by, as a random example, a passing hiker, then you are safe. There is no way, though, to know whether the leaves against which you have just rubbed are compromised—until it's too late.

One of the other things about poison ivy is that urushiol is water soluble. So, if you can take a dip shortly after contact, then the acid can be washed off. As the canyon at this point was completely dry, I hurried down the trail, hoping to make it to Hutch's Pool as soon as possible. I actually began running, which made it hard to keep my eyes peeled for rattlers. Every time I saw a stick on or near the trail, my heart missed several very important beats. It would be my luck to get bit because I was running down the trail in hopes of heading off a case of poison ivy. I could just hear the folks back in Summerhaven—who had warned me in the strongest of terms to keep my eyes peeled for snakes—laughing at the thought.

"*The sky was completely clear, and the surrounding pine forest was snow covered from where I stood all the way to the summit of Mount Lemmon.*"

I could hear Hutch's Pool long before I arrived. Not that it was making any noise. It was too tranquil for that. Rather, it was the massive Boy Scout troop camped next to the pool that caught my auditory attention, as well as, I'm sure, the attention of people more than 100 miles away. There was a serious rock-skipping competition going on, and the Scouts were not shy about vocalizing their opinions on the relative quality of the various tosses.

Without even stopping to say howdy, I sprinted to a place where I could drop my pack. From there, I stripped, jumped into the tannin-stained pool, and washed vigorously, hoping against hope that whatever poison ivy

Riparian zone in Bear Canyon, Santa Catalina Mountains
❖❖❖

View of the Santa Catalina Mountains from Agua Caliente Canyon

❖❖❖

Grasslands with the Rincon Mountains in the distance, Coronado National Forest

◆ ◆ ◆

slime I might have on me was being diluted into nothingness. Only after I had scrubbed two layers of skin away did I return to my pack. I soon found a delightful campsite, and as I was setting up my tent, I realized, sadly, that the entire area was infested with—you guessed it—poison ivy. I would have to move about very carefully. But even as I thought that thought, I knew I was doomed. I might as well go over and roll around in the middle of the thickest patch of poison ivy and face the inevitable.

"During that descent, which was spread out over 5 miles, I went from snow to saguaros. It was like driving from Canada to Mexico in sixty minutes."

After a double-portion dinner of curried rice and chicken with some extra rice and chicken, I sat against a large rock and watched the evening settle in. The canyon was several thousand feet deep, and the canyon walls sported lots of nice saguaros.

I did not get a ton of sleep, as the nearby Boy Scouts were apparently working on their bellowing merit badge. There's nothing wrong with boys being boys in the woods. May they be inclined to be exuberant in the wilderness for their rest of their lives.

THE CLIMB INTO THE Rincon Mountains of Saguaro National Park two days later was the single hardest day of my entire AZT trip. It was only 14 miles from Redington Road to Manning Camp—one of the official campgrounds in the park. The night before, I had sat next to my tent on the side of Redington Road, stared up at the Rincon Mountains, which top out at about 8,000 feet, and convinced myself that they looked fairly benign. I thought it likely that I would make it to Manning Camp without breaking a sweat. No such luck. The hike beat me to death.

What I did not count on was a trail that was obviously designed before switchbacks were invented. This torturous stretch of path blasted straight up the north side of the range for more than 5 miles, gaining almost 4,000 feet.

Ancient, twisted saguaro cactus
◆.◆.◆

Morning light on saguaro cactus, Saguaro National Park

❖❖❖

View of the Rincon Mountains, Coronado National Forest

❖❖❖

I kept expecting the trail to integrate itself into some of the nearby beautiful rock formations, but it would have none of it. This was a trail on a mission, and aesthetics were not part of that mission. Its goal was to get to the top of the Rincons as quickly and directly as possible. By the time I got to Italian Spring, I felt like I could go no farther, and I do not think that thought often.

Almost immediately thereafter, I found myself hiking in ankle-deep snow, making my progress even more laborious. There were no tracks in the snow, yet it most certainly fell from the same weather front that nailed me in Oracle five nights earlier. No one had been up here in that time.

It got down to 20°F that night, and there was a thick frost on my tent as I packed up the following morning. I only had a 10-mile downhill day to Miller Canyon Trailhead planned, and I got to my truck by noon. From this point there is a 36-mile gap in the AZT, so I drove 16 miles to Interstate 10, along a pleasantly rutted dirt road. Along the way, it hit me: Only one more section of the AZT lay before me.

Saguaro blossoms
◆.◆.◆

Saguaro National Park
to the Mexican Border

❖.❖.❖.❖.❖.❖.❖.❖.❖.❖.❖

I HAD LEFT MY TRUCK at a motel in the lovely town of Patagonia, and Jay Scott (one of my oldest and dearest buddies from my college days in Silver City, New Mexico) was going to bring me around to a point where Cienega Creek crosses Interstate 10. This is one of those sections where the trail is still several years away from being completed, so between the interstate and the Coronado National Forest boundary some 20 miles south, there essentially is no AZT. There is only a vague set of directions to "follow Cienega Creek as far as Empire Ranch." Easy enough, I was told, because there is a dirt road that follows the creek the entire way.

So, I had a relaxed 13-mile day planned, and I asked Jay to pull over at some godforsaken place called the Empirita Interchange. According to my map, we were only a mile or so from Cienega Creek, and there appeared to be a dirt road heading off in the proper direction.

"Are you sure this is it?" Jay queried.

"If there is one thing I have learned on this trail, it is to not be sure of anything," I responded, laying a serious abrazo on my amigo before we parted ways.

Jay stood by his car as I walked away down a sorry excuse for a dirt road toward the railroad tracks that parallel Interstate 10. Two seconds after Jay pulled away, I came across a no-nonsense set of signs basically letting me know that if I even *considered* trespassing on this property, I would be tarred, feathered, lectured, chastised, and then prosecuted to the full extent of the law.

What was I to do? I am a firm believer in landowners having the right to tell people like me to stay the hell off their property. But I was between a rock and a hard place here. I followed the fence around to the north, hoping to be able to bypass the private property altogether. Then I walked directly on the railroad tracks to a point that I felt certain was beyond the private property boundary. Unfortunately, I came across a new set of signs, these telling me that I was about to enter the Cienega Creek Research Conservation Area, and that I needed a permit to tromp upon this particular land—for reasons that were never entirely clear.

I have far less compunction about trespassing on government land than I do about trespassing on private land, so I opened the gate, walked through, and crossed my fingers. At least I was now directly in the Cienega Creek drainage, which was dry as a bone. No creek to this particular creek, at least at this point.

A mile later I came to yet another set of bright-red No Trespassing signs. I was back on the ranch that I had just spent so much time and energy skirting. Faced with a rather limited set of alternatives, I clambered over the barbed-wire fence and hoped that I would not soon be making the acquaintance of any steely-eyed cowboys wanting to know who I was and what I was doing there.

Just when I got to the point where I thought I was home free on the private property front, I rounded a bend and found myself standing smack dead in the middle of someone's front yard. There was nothing for me to do,

❖.❖.❖

Sunset over Red Mountain, view from Canelo Hills

Yucca against the setting sun, Empire-Cienega Ranch Conservation Area

◆◆◆

Sunset, Empire-Cienega Ranch Conservation Area

◆◆◆

Cottonwood grove along Cienega Creek
◆◆◆

save put my hands in my pockets, innocently whistle a song, and stride by like I had every right in the world to be where I was. I have no idea if anyone saw me.

The road starting forking and intersecting other roads, and I made a couple of wrong directional guesses. There were no road markers and certainly no AZT signs, and I started getting flustered a little more quickly than usual. I pulled out my maps, but my brain was refusing to translate the information they contained into a language I could use. A couple of times I even got my basic ordinal directions and my lefts and rights backward, causing numerous teeth-gnashing backtrackings. It was hot, but not hot enough to disorient me like this. I was growing more short-tempered by the minute, and that reality was exacerbated by the fact that I was getting nervous about the water situation. I was told that 6 miles south of the interstate, beginning at a place called "The Narrows," Cienega Creek was actually supposed to boast a flow. The farther I walked, the less it looked like this particular wash was going to get wet. My skepticism was beginning to dominate my thought processes; it was now my operative emotion.

Soon I was trying to predict which of the so-far unimpressive geologic features lining the creek was going to call itself The Narrows. According to the map, it looked like it gained its name via a modest boxing up of Cienega Creek and was something like 50 feet deep and 100 feet across—topographically unimpressive statistics, but significant enough to force a detour of the track on which I was walking in an area where several dirt roads come together within a half-mile span. I exited onto one likely-looking candidate and ended up grunting my way up a steep hill for 30 minutes, until that road curved off to the north—the exact opposite direction I wanted to go.

As I was grumbling and growling, I heard what I thought, at first, was wind making its way through the trees. Then I realized it was the sound of moving water. I broke through some thick undergrowth down to the creek and, sure enough, it was flowing—impressively. I had expected that if there was going to be any water at all in Cienega Creek it would be found in small, semi-stagnant pools. There were actually numerous fish swimming around. I must have spent five full minutes looking down at the water then up at the landscape. Nothing had changed topographically, yet now there was all this agua. Strange indeed.

Sunflowers, Empire-Cienega Ranch Conservation Area
◆◆◆

Heartened, I enthusiastically hiked a quick mile down yet another wrong dirt road, this one eventually heading due east, toward the Whetstone Mountains. When I returned from this little detour, I opted to take the one remaining road within a 100-mile radius that I had not yet followed off in a wrong direction. It led me in short order to The Narrows, which ended up being a wonderful place that had deep pools, grassy banks, and shaded shores. I would have loved to have hung out for a few hours, but all my directional befuddlements had burned whatever discretionary dillydallying I could do this day. So, after pausing only long enough to wet my bandanna and rinse my face, I hightailed it down yet another wrong dirt road for yet another wasted half hour. Fuming, I returned to The Narrows only to observe the obvious road I should have seen the first time around. This road climbed up and around on the west side of The Narrows, just like the map told me it would.

> **"As I was grumbling and growling, I heard what I thought, at first, was wind making its way through the trees. Then I realized it was the sound of moving water."**

I spent the next three hours going from one wrong road to the next. Finally, in utter exasperation, I took a compass bearing and struck out cross-country, through the mesquite-infested hills toward Empire Ranch, which—at this rate—I ought to arrive at sometime in the year 3045.

At least the distant views were awe inspiring. To the west and southwest lay the Santa Rita Mountains, with 9,453-foot Mount Wrightson and its namesake wilderness area (through which I would be passing in four days) dominating the range. To the north, the Rincons still filled the horizon. Remembering how badly they had kicked my butt, I shuddered even to look at that particular range. But look at them I did, because they are visible almost all the way to the Mexican border. To the east were the wild-looking Whetstones, and to the south, the steep Patagonias. This was some seriously rugged mountain country.

Sunburst through a mesquite tree, Empire-Cienega Ranch Conservation Area
◆◆◆

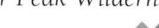

Although it was tough busting my way through the flesh-ripping mesquite forest, at least it was now fairly easy to remain oriented. The cottonwood trees along Cienega Creek were huge and golden. I tried to stay high enough on the surrounding hills to avoid the tightly vegetated riparian zone, but close enough that I did not venture too far away from what was going to be my water source when I finally made camp.

As the sun began to dip behind the Santa Ritas, I started thinking in terms of finding a campsite pronto. I could not believe that I was going to fall short of my day's goal when I only had 13 miles planned. I hiked toward the creek and found sheer, 30-foot-high banks with no place to hike down to the water. I went back and forth for twenty minutes and could find no access point, so I returned, red faced, to my slog toward Empire Ranch.

> **"*To the east were the wild-looking Whetstones,
> and to the south, the steep Patagonias. This was
> some seriously rugged mountain country.*"**

At long last I came upon a windmill. I knew that I was supposed to pass by a ranch house, but the map did not indicate its state of repair or whether it would be occupied. Then I saw several vehicles and a house that looked like it was home sweet home for someone. I dropped my pack, ambled over to the gate and yelled a greeting. I was soon chatting with a lady named LuAnn. She and her husband took their responsibilities as the only residents for miles very seriously. They had an outside spigot with a note telling passersby to help themselves, and they had a public emergency phone. LuAnn not only pointed the way toward Empire Ranch, but she handed me a copy of the map she and her husband "give to everyone who gets lost here." She allowed me to fill my water bottles and water bag, which was good because, despite what I had been told, Cienega Creek was now completely dry again.

Since it was getting late, I planned to hike just out of sight of the house before placing my tent on the first level patch of ground I came across. As I walked back to my pack, I pondered the entire concept of

An Emory oak clings to a rocky hillside, Canelo Hills
❖❖❖

"being lost," which LuAnn obviously thought I was. Now, I have been lost more than my fair share of times, and I am not ashamed to admit that I can get turned around as well as the next man. However, being lost includes two components: not knowing where you are and not knowing how to get to where you want to be. Once I came across the ranch house, I knew exactly where I was. I just did not know exactly how to get to Empire Ranch—but I was not lost. Really. I swear. At least by the definition I have invented for myself.

I found a pleasant, tree-lined campsite right next to the dirt road on which I would be walking the following day. It was five o'clock—the latest I arrived in camp since leaving Utah. I could not believe I had had such a bad day, and after dinner I forced myself to think about why. I have always been a firm believer that there is little justification for being in a foul mood while hiking and camping in the great outdoors.

No matter how hard I tried, I could come up with no reason or excuse for being in such a bad mood. As I sat there in the warm evening, the last rays of sunlight made both the Santa Ritas and the Whetstones turn bright red. Several flocks of birds of indeterminate lineage flew overhead, and a nearby herd of cattle grazed in the middle of a perfectly bucolic postcard scene. I generally hate having bovines muddle up a vista, but this particular herd in this particular place seemed to fit. Then a mental light bulb turned on: This wonderful trip was fast drawing to a close, and I was sad about that. That sadness was translating itself into today's foul humor.

Despite the challenge the AZT had presented, or perhaps because of that challenge, I was loathe to part ways with this trail, this experience, this part of the country. I was now perfectly comfortable with the straightforward simplicity of trail life—the long days, darkness descending at 6 PM, the monotonous food that was tasting better and better every day—and I knew I was not yet ready to abandon that life in favor of a return to Grim Reality. But there was nothing I could do about that. Trails end. And when they end, you have to move on to other adventures. It's that simple. The only thing you can do is savor every moment you have on a trail and try hard to bring as much of that trail and of your experience on that trail back home with you.

I was glad to have scheduled in a series of short days for this last stretch. Gave me time to establish a context for my return to civilization. I

Maple trees showing spectacular fall color, Miller Peak Wilderness
◆◆◆

arrived at my next water cache, which was in a lovely stand of oak alongside Highway 90, at 11:30 AM. The next day, I got to Kentucky Camp by noon, and the last day before arriving in Patagonia, I had camp set up at Bear Spring, in Mount Wrightson Wilderness, by one in the afternoon. I spent those afternoons smoking cigars, reading, writing in my journal, and just thinking about my life when I left the AZT.

> "*Despite the challenge the AZT had presented, or perhaps because of that challenge, I was loathe to part ways with this trail, this experience, this part of the country.*"

Perhaps I was too fixated on the fact that, within a week, I would be trading in my pack for a briefcase, but the thing about a long adventure of any kind—and particularly an arduous, self-propelled adventure—is that you are obligated karmically to grow as a person as a result of the journey. You have to return to real life somehow changed for the better, otherwise there is no sense in having done the trip in the first place. Seeking experience for the sake of experience is a perfectly valid enterprise, but there has to be more to it than that.

Generally, when I am on a long hike, I handle this growing-as-a-person thing by establishing one part-objective, part-subjective, part-palpable, part-nebulous goal on returning home. When I completed the Appalachian Trail in 1980, I determined it was time to quit talking about becoming a writer and actually become a writer. I returned to college and, before graduating, got my first newspaper gig. When I completed the Colorado Trail in 1991, I made it my goal to take up serious study of the martial arts, which I did and still do. When I completed the Colorado section of the Continental Divide Trail in 1996, I decided to quit thinking of outdoor writing as something to do until I start writing about "more serious subjects." I decided to follow my heart instead of my ego, and embrace outdoor writing like the friend and benefactor it was, is, and likely always will be.

View of San Jose Mountain from near the Mexican border
◆.◆.◆

Now I was nearing the end of my two-month hike along the AZT, and it was time to adopt a posthike lifestyle goal. To be successful, though, this cannot be anything artificial. It has to be something you really and truly want, and are willing and able to work for and achieve. And it has to be something fairly large. Fortunately, the mind-set is easy, because this is a time when you can tell yourself honestly: If you can do this hike, you can do pretty much anything.

As I walked the last 17 miles from Mount Wrightson Wilderness into Patagonia, I stopped my introspective marathon dead in its tracks with one last thought. I have pretty much known since the day I hiked into the Superstition Wilderness what my post-AZT lifestyle goal would be: to buy into the concept of voluntary simplicity; to start living lighter and leaner on the land when I return home.

IT OCCURS TO ME that I've been thinking entirely too much lately. It was time to stop ruminating and start savoring the last aesthetic morsels of my AZT hike. This was not hard to do, as the terrain hereabouts was stunning. After the aspen-filled remoteness of the Arizona strip, the incomparable depths of the Grand Canyon, the snow-covered San Francisco Peaks, the Mogollon Rim, the Mazatzals, Reavis Creek, and the Catalinas, it was hard for me to determine which part of Arizona I liked most; but, if forced to make a decision, I believe I would have to go with the southernmost reaches of the state. Here, the dry grass is thick, waist high, and the oak woods are gorgeous. This is Arizona's wine-producing region and, true to form, it looked like something out of Italy or Spain.

From the road that led into town, I could almost see into Mexico. This is some of the least tame country in the Lower Forty-eight. Jay had given me a copy of a magazine article dealing with the fact that *jaguars*—the third-largest feline in the world—had reintroduced themselves into this exact area. I had not known that jaguars ever lived here, but they did, and now they do again. It is thrilling to think that a place wild enough to support jaguars still exists in the continental United States.

I spent one night in Patagonia, during which time I exercised poor judgment by visiting both of the town's watering holes. The main topic of conversation that night was that a fierce storm was expected to move in, and

it was expected to last more than a week. As I was driving in my last supply caches early the next morning, the sky turned steely gray and the wind picked up. It was getting cold fast. I left my truck at a trailhead overlooking Parker Canyon Lake and spent the rest of the day hitchhiking back to Patagonia.

> "*After the aspen-filled remoteness of the Arizona strip, the incomparable depths of the Grand Canyon, the snow-covered San Francisco Peaks, the Mogollon Rim, the Mazatzals, Reavis Creek, and the Catalinas, it was hard for me to determine which part of Arizona I liked the most.*"

It took me two days to hike through the rolling Canelo Hills, past Gate Spring, and over Canelo Pass back to my truck. By that time, the weather was subatrocious. I left my truck and hiked less than 3 miles—my shortest day on the entire AZT—to Scotia Canyon, at the foot of the mighty Huachuca Mountain Range. The next day I was set to hike up and over Miller Peak, which is almost 10,000 feet high, before dropping into Montezuma Pass, on the western edge of Coronado National Memorial—only 4 miles from the Mexican border.

This was to be my last night on the AZT and, even though the setting was splendid—great views, beautiful woods—the weather was so foul I was in my tent by 4:30. It poured all night, and several times I thought my little Sierra Designs Flash Magic was going to blow away with me in it.

By dawn, it was obvious that I would not be hiking 19 miles through Miller Peak Wilderness to Montezuma Pass. The cloud level was down to 5,000 feet and it was nasty. I heard later that this was one of the worst November storms to ravage southeastern Arizona in years. Deep snow was predicted up on the Miller Peak Crest Trail, which the AZT follows. I did not have enough food to wait this weather out, so I hid my pack, hiked back to Parker Canyon Lake, got my truck, drove back around to pick up my

One mile from the southern terminus of the trail

◆ ◆ ◆

belongings at Scotia Canyon, and hightailed it to Coronado National Memorial headquarters, where I was told by the Park Service people that the AZT from Montezuma Pass to the Mexican border was closed because trail crews were using dynamite to blast through some rock formations.

I could not believe this sudden turn of events. After hiking from Utah, I was unable to complete my trek to Mexico. Fortunately the Park Service people told me about a nearby dirt road on which I could walk the last mile to the border. I drove to that road and hiked through the frigid, driving rain to the barbed-wire fence marking the end of the United States and the beginning of old Mexico. I have spent so much time in Mexico that I almost feel as comfortable there as I do in my own country. It was hard to turn around and head back north, but I had to be home by December 1, lest I lose my job, and it was now the day before Thanksgiving. I did not have time to go into Mexico. I did not have time to wait this storm out and hike through Miller Peak Wilderness. I only had time to drive home.

On the way back to my truck, I was struck by an intense and chilling thought: *I'd better keep my eyes peeled for jaguars!*

"... the thing about a long adventure of any kind ...
is that you are obligated karmically to grow as a person
as a result of the journey. You have to return to real life
somehow changed for the better, otherwise there is no
sense in having done the trip in the first place."

WHAT IS THE ARIZONA TRAIL?

THE ARIZONA TRAIL (AZT) is a continuous, 750-mile nonmotorized corridor through Arizona—reaching from Utah to Mexico—linking deserts, mountains, and canyons. But the AZT is more than just a line connecting two points on a map. The AZT represents a community—a community committed to provide you with the experience of traversing the pristine beauty of Arizona's spectacular landscapes and of delving into the rich natural heritage of nearby historical and cultural sites. The AZT is for anyone who loves the outdoors, including hikers, backpackers, equestrians, mountain bikers, and cross-country skiers. All are afforded the opportunity to enjoy the activities the AZT provides: Traveling through seven life zones—from the saguaros of the Sonoran Desert to the coniferous forests found at higher elevations; viewing the magnificent variety of wildlife; climbing mountains like the Huachuca, Santa Rita, Superstition, Rincon, Santa Catalina, and the San Francisco Peaks; and tracing the steps of Native American tribes, early explorers, and pioneers along historic routes—just to name a few.

How did the AZT come about and who is making it happen? The AZT was the idea of Flagstaff teacher and hiking enthusiast Dale Shewalter. His vision was to develop a long-distance trail that would highlight Arizona's topographic, biologic, historic, and cultural diversity. Today, his modest dream is becoming a reality as more and more people have seen the potential for a trail that traverses the entire length of the state. Every day, work is accomplished on the AZT by the Arizona Trail Association, which represents a growing number of people from all over the nation—and the world—who support efforts to build and maintain the AZT.

The Arizona Trail Association was created in 1994 by a group of dedicated individuals who represented various trail interests. These efforts continue today with even more energy and dedication. Numerous agencies and groups work with the Arizona Trail Association in helping to complete the trail, including Arizona State Parks, Bureau of Land Management, U.S. Forest Service, National Park Service, Sierra Club, Arizona State Committee on Trails, and many other state, county, and city organizations. Private businesses, youth and educational groups, and recreational organizations also play crucial roles. Yet much of the most important work is done by individuals—people from all walks of life who love the outdoors. These dedicated individuals not only want to be able to enjoy the AZT themselves, but also want to ensure the quality of the AZT for future generations. Members of the Arizona Trail Association participate in trail construction and maintenance, publicity, fund-raising, education, research, and stewardship of the AZT. Trail stewards—individuals and groups—work to ensure that the AZT is well managed and properly maintained for continued recreational and educational use.

The Arizona Trail Association works in many ways: one is promotional. We get the word out that the AZT is a unique and outstanding recreational and educational resource within the state of Arizona. Another important part of our work is to provide opportunities for outdoor enthusiasts to become involved in AZT planning, construction, and maintenance. Recently, thirty-five eager volunteers celebrated National Trail Day by working on the Blue Ridge Passage—a trail that connects the AZT to the Rock Crossing Campground near the Blue Ridge Ranger District. A group of Boy Scouts was joined by members of the Sierra Club. The day was a huge success, and a great deal of fun as well. Projects like this demonstrate the energy and enthusiasm for the AZT.

One of the most important aspects of our work is education. We provide trail users with helpful information about completed AZT sections. We publish the *Arizona Trail News* quarterly, and use this medium to keep our members informed of the latest in trail news and events. Recent accomplishments of the Arizona Trail Association include the completion of more than 2,000 hours of trail and trailhead construction, the appointment of new stewards, and the development of outreach programs.

Won't you join us in our efforts? Help us maintain the integrity of the AZT by participating in the excitement of developing this significant recreational and cultural project. We need your participation as a part of the collective of hikers, backpackers, equestrians, mountain bikers, and other nonmotorized trail users in planning and constructing the AZT. We count on the active support of people like you—people who enjoy the outdoors and who care about our natural environment. The AZT is being built for you, your family, and your friends to enjoy. Help us to build this resource for today, and to provide a legacy for future generations.

Memberships may be purchased annually as follows: $15 for students and seniors, $25 for individuals or families, and $100 for Trailblazer memberships. Lifetime memberships are $500, and a Trail Patron membership is $1,000. Organizations are also eligible for membership at varying rates. Your financial support, in any amount, is critical. Additional contributions for AZT development are greatly appreciated (dues as well as contributions are tax deductible). For more information, write the Arizona Trail Association at P.O. Box 36736, Phoenix, AZ 85067; call (602)-252-4794; or email ata@aztrail.org. Visit our website at www.primenet.com/~aztrail.

From the ancient rocks of the Mazatzal Wilderness to the colossal wonder of the Grand Canyon, the AZT links landscapes and people. We invite everyone to be a part of the development, support, and enjoment of the AZT. It is *your* trail! Join us now, get involved, and be an important part of the link. *Arizona Trail*

Along *the* Arizona Trail

AREA DETAILED

ARIZONA

FLAGSTAFF

PHOENIX

TUCSON

0 10 20 30 40 50

Miles

N

H

A

R

I

Z

A

R

I

Z

O

N

A

U

T

160

163

160

40

Painted Desert

Mogollon Rim

TUBA CITY

Mormon Lake

Pine

San Francisco Peaks
(12,633 ft.)

EAST VERDE RIVER

LAKE POWELL

PAGE

89

89

Kachina Peaks Wilderness

FLAGSTAFF

CHAPTER 3

GLEN CANYON NATIONAL RECREATION AREA

89

CHAPTER 2

Coconino National Forest

SEDONA

WINSLOW

64

40

VERDE RIVER

Utah–Arizona border
(Northern terminus of the Arizona Trail)

ALT 89

CHAPTER 1

GRAND CANYON NATIONAL PARK

North Rim Village

Phantom Ranch

South Rim Village

180

64

Kaibab National Forest

WILLIAMS

PRESCOTT NATIONAL FOREST

89

Jacob Lake

67

89

COLORADO RIVER

ALT 89

40

17

89

PRESCOTT

PRESCOTT NATIONAL FOREST

66